A LIFE OF ADORATION

"The Eucharistic liturgy is a pre-eminent school of Christian prayer for the community. The Mass opens up a wide variety of possibilities for a sound pedagogy of the spirit. One of these is Adoration of the Blessed Sacrament, which is a natural prolongation of the Eucharistic celebration. Through Adoration, the faithful can enjoy a particular experience of 'abiding' in the love of Christ (cf. Jn 15:9), entering evermore deeply into his filial relationship with the Father."

Letter of the Holy Father Pope John Paul II
to priests, for Holy Thursday 1999

MARIE-BENOÎTE ANGOT

A Life of Adoration

Translated by
Heather Buttery

ST PAULS

Original Title: *La vie d'adoration*
Translated from the French
Translated by Heather Buttery

ST PAULS Publishing
187 Battersea Bridge Road, London SW11 3AS, UK
www.stpauls.ie

Copyright (English Translation) © ST PAULS UK 2002

ISBN 085439 640 3

Set by Tukan DTP, Fareham, UK
Printed by Interprint Ltd, Marsa, Malta

ST PAULS is an activity of the priests and brothers of
the Society of St Paul who proclaim the Gospel
through the media of social communication

Contents

Introduction   9

1 **Adoration and life**   13
    An impulse of pure love   15

    Looking   24
      Adoring Jesus is looking at him lovingly   24
      Total commitment   26
      God is gazing upon us   30

    Changing our lives   35
      Conversion   36
      Transformation   43
      Transfiguration   48

2 **The life within us**   51
    Adoration and the interior life   51

    Adoration and the Evangelical life   61
      Listening to the Word of God   64
      Respecting the Word of God   66

    Love in Adoration, a path of holiness for our time   76

3	**Christ, our life**	76
	Christ, the only source of holiness	76
	Discovering the person of Christ	77
	Love in adoration: the special pathway to a meeting with God	79
	The person of Christ is unique	83
	The manifestations of Christ	84
	Christ in his Eucharistic presence is the link	85
	The Body and Blood of Christ, the only pathway	92
	The Traditional Passover	97
	The New Passover	98
	The Third Passover	99
4	**Eternal Adoration**	106
	The Lamb	106
	The Lamb of the Old Testament	107
	Christ, Lamb of God	109
	The Lamb of God is linked to the Eucharist and to our adoration	112
	The Lamb of Revelation	114
	The Body of Christ and its eternal wounds	116
	The Immaculate Lamb	119
	The wedding joy, a state of overwhelming happiness	123

5 **A love to be lived in our homes** 129
The importance of the home in the life
of Jesus 129

The importance of Houses of Adoration in
the new evangelisation 132

The house in the Old Testament 133

The house at the heart of the New Covenant 134

Houses of Adoration, needed so much today 135

Domestic churches, extensions of the Church
in the world around us 137

Houses of Adoration, a Eucharistic vocation
in the everyday world 138

Houses of Adoration, forerunners of the
Holy City 142

Introduction

*"One God alone will you adore,
and love above all else."*[1]

If we want to make progress in our spiritual life and ensure that our intimate relationship with Christ becomes ever deeper and stronger, we need to reflect upon the real meaning of adoration. Chapters 1 and 2 will develop the theme of what adoration is, and why we should practice adoration.

Following on from the Creation, ordained for the adoration of the Creator, mankind received this first commandment revealing the kind of relationship to be enjoyed with God.

Adoration is thus part of the nature of a human being, written into our hearts by God himself. It is the impulse of the soul by which a creature turns towards his creator, in a loving response to Living Love.

Adoration is the name given to that intimate exchange between mankind and God. It is the outpouring of love which mankind sends to him, and keeps sending, in return for the existence and being drawn from him.

Adoring or worshipping, and loving, are closely linked. God himself, talking to Moses, brought out the connection between these two concepts, showing mankind not only a spiritual path, but the true path to holiness. We are talking about a power of love, a power of life, a power of love to be lived. This is not just any kind of love. Linked with adoration, it is directed towards God alone. This is **love in adoration**, an expression which brings together both the love and the adoration due to God:

- a strong spiritual impulse which, from the depths of the heart of mankind, soars up to God,
- a perfect and direct pathway of holiness, given by God himself from the earliest days.

God himself wanted to engrave love and adoration not only on the Tablets of the Law given into the care of Moses, but also into the depths of man's heart: *they shall be my people, and I will be their God.*²

In order to understand the importance of adoration, we need to know what we are adoring, or rather, whom we are adoring (cf. chapter 3). At this dawn of the third millennium, have we truly understood love in adoration as a path to holiness? Are we aware, when we consider Jesus' striking comparison in the Gospel concerning Jonas, that we have amongst us far more than Moses had? We have Jesus-Eucharist, **present** and **living** in the midst of mankind.

The full significance of the words **loving** and **adoring** depends upon the object loved or adored. We can love any number of unusual and assorted things. We can even say we adore them but this has hardly any meaning anymore, and even less conviction. We love and adore chocolate just as much as holidays, biking or music. It is therefore time to bring these words back into a single phrase so that we can rediscover their deeper meaning and their full power.

If the Living God, who revealed himself to the succession of great prophets as the God of our fathers, is worthy of love and adoration to such an extent that he made them one of life's commandments, then surely Jesus, the Son of the Father, is also worthy of them? Love and adoration should all the more direct our lives unceasingly towards Jesus-Eucharist, the Son of God, and God himself given to mankind.

Love in adoration is the strongest tie which can bind us to our God, and the Living God in the midst of mankind is for us, at this point in history, Jesus-Eucharist.

Adoration thus enables us to discover the person of Christ and, more precisely, Christ himself living in his Eucharist by the force of the Spirit. By means of a never-ending interchange, as little by little we discover Jesus-Eucharist living amongst us, we find our love and adoration for him growing intensely.

This is what we will experience in all its fullness in the Kingdom, when we come into it.

A life of adoration is an anticipation of eternal life. Experienced here in this life, it sets us off on the path of happiness which Jesus promises us in the Gospel, but which, once again, we only understand in anticipation. All we have is a foretaste. The real magnitude of this happiness will only be revealed to us in the Kingdom, where we will exist in a state of eternal adoration (cf. chapter 4). This is the sure basis of our joyful expectations.

Let us pray that many souls will live a life of adoration at this start of the third millennium, so that the Church may grow and achieve her ultimate splendour, and that Christ may manifest his glory in that long-awaited third Passover.

NOTES

1. Traditional catechetical formula in France, summarising the First Commandment and resembling Mt 4:10. See Ex 20:2-17; Deut 5:6-21 and also the *Catechism of the Catholic Church*, no. 2052
2. Lev 26:12; Ezek 11:20.

1
Adoration and life

"Look to him, and be radiant."[1]

Love in adoration is the response to a calling sent out to us by the Lord, a calling which he invites us to live in the everyday world and through which he draws us irresistibly towards him. The Lord himself pulls us towards him in the love and adoration of his person.

Love in adoration is thus not just any kind of love: centred in adoration, it is entirely directed towards the Living God: Father, Son and Holy Spirit. We are talking about experiencing something very special. It seems to me that it involves not only the discovery of the most exalted form of love in all its delicacy but also all its force.

From the very beginning, adoration of the Eucharist takes us much further than prayer of intercession, prayer of praise, or prayer of petition. It might be very good to start with these: it is not a question of replacing or eliminating these different forms of prayer which we often use. They also allow us to place all our cares at Jesus' feet. But they are all only small stages in the journey towards a greater union with God.

What the Lord really wants is to lead us much further, so we become **souls of adoration** in the everyday world. He wants to make us realise that love in adoration is an act of 'pure love'. The word 'act' is not to be taken to mean an action. Its precise sense here is the involvement of all our being, letting ourselves be taken over by Jesus who himself acts through us. It is more helpful to say that the act of pure love is an impulse which rushes out from all our being in order to align itself, like the needle on a compass, with the living person of Christ. It is like a current of pure love between the soul and the living person of Jesus. We make contact, we meet up in that great embrace: the meeting of the soul with Jesus.

At the same time, a very strong but very delicate person-to-person link is created. Through love in adoration, our poor, feeble and fragile human person finds itself intimately bound up with the living person of Christ in the Eucharist. And that changes everything for us, for the link connecting us to Jesus allows us to receive the very force of his love into all our being. Jesus does not only become present in our soul through the miracle of the Eucharist, but in our flesh, too.

We are now touching upon an essential element of our existence, for if the dignity which is part of our human person is to find its source and reach its full potential, it can only be through this supreme and intimate encounter with Christ. He is, *par excellence*, the perfect model for every human being.

This is something which people today need to realise, for the true happiness which all human beings aspire to with all their force and which cannot be found outside Christ, exists only in this encounter. No human being can discover the meaning of his destiny unless he is linked up to the person of the resurrected Christ who, through the Incarnation, was born of the flesh of the Virgin Mary, and who through the Eucharist, transforms and gives life to our flesh!

The mystery of the Eucharist is at the heart of our lives, of the life of our body and soul, of our entire being. It is at the heart of our earthly existence, in order to lead us to a life of glory. This is why it is vital to live this Eucharistic mystery, finding it both **in the heart of the Church and in the heart of the everyday world.** It is up to each of us to do so as soon as we can.

An impulse of pure love

An impulse of pure love can best be explained by the following example. It comes from one of the Gospel scenes: the spontaneous gesture of Mary of Bethany towards Jesus (Jn 12:1-8). We must immerse ourselves in this passage in order to understand what the Lord expects from us.

Jesus is there in the house of Lazarus, surrounded by his apostles and by people who have come to listen to him. Suddenly Mary approaches Jesus and pours precious perfumed ointment over his feet. She then wipes his feet dry with her long hair. We all know this passage well.

This woman's spontaneous gesture expresses the impulse of pure love drawing her to Jesus. She has asked no one for permission to do it. But still, she dares to pour this precious perfume over the feet of her Lord and her Master. Such a gesture on the part of a woman during those times contravened all notions of propriety. It was an audacious thing to do to a man, all the more so because the man in question was acknowledged to be the Master and the Lord. *He spoke with authority*, the Gospel tells us.

So Mary dares to carry out this act which would seem to be pure folly, but she is letting herself be guided by love. It is a prayer, and much more than a prayer. Accompanied by a conversion of the heart and a request for forgiveness, the prayer becomes that 'act' we spoke of earlier, a gesture of affection and a vital impulse of adoration. By doing this, she wants to tell Jesus that she wishes to serve him. She will stand by him forever, she is there to serve him. Her act is in anticipation of the washing of the feet, and Jesus accepts her gesture, since she has already understood that to love is to become a servant. She wants to indicate that her whole self is at the service of the person of Jesus, in an impulse of pure love which takes her a long, long way. She has grasped the fact that Jesus, in his human person, needs this token of love before he suffers his Passion. She is perhaps the only person – apart from the Blessed Virgin, silently, we can be sure – to feel profoundly the immense suffering of Jesus as his Passion approaches. The apostles themselves, who are all around Jesus, find it difficult to understand this imminent mystery of the Passion. Jesus has prepared them for it, but it seems unthinkable. The hour approaches, however, and Jesus is facing it very much on his own. A woman, Mary, has understood, and empathises with Jesus, kneeling at his feet. She has become one with the suffering person of Christ. A great deal of love and adoration are necessary for this to happen.

Mary of Bethany believes that Jesus is the Son of God who brought her brother Lazarus back to life. This woman's gratitude and love stem from that which she has recognised in the person of Jesus, the Son of the Living God. No one can say which is stronger, her love or her adoration, but we can be certain that the two are intermingled. Mary loves the person of Jesus with an impulse of pure love, and she also adores him. She loves him as God who has come to give up his life to save us. So she does not hesitate to step forward, to take the initiative and take care of him.

What a marvellous story it is, this woman's encounter with Jesus. It's a person-to-person and heart-to-heart meeting. Love in adoration, which is flowing out of the woman's heart and finding expression in this spontaneous gesture of pure love, brings her instantly into the mystery of God, into the discovery of Jesus, Son of God made man. Her grateful love and her love in adoration bring her instantly into the mystery of Salvation: in other words, into the mystery of suffering, of the Passion, of the absolute gift which Jesus is making of his person, a gift which saves mankind from sin and death. This in itself is a kind of Eucharist in the form of thanksgiving. Jesus, who knows the depths of our hearts, reveals what lies deep in this woman's heart when he says: *She bought it so that she might keep it for the day of my burial* (Jn 12:7). Dismissing all the criticisms, Jesus thus condones the gesture and explains it. He gives it a purpose.

But Jesus' approval includes at the same time a sense of admiration and gratitude, for there is no doubt that this expression of love and adoration has meant a great deal to him. In the midst of the anguish which he is facing alone as his Passion approaches, a woman takes pains to take care of him, and to offer him some consolation.

We see here the delicacy of the love which keeps silent, but which is lived. There is a mysterious link connecting the two hearts together, enabling them to reach each other and penetrate far into the most intimate depths of each, knowing that which is most secret, and therefore most precious. Love alone can permit such understanding, such a journey into mystery, into everything which is hidden from others. This is the nature of love in adoration: it is the love which we bring to our Living God. This love carries us along with it until we find his person, propelling us right to the heart of his mystery, to the most intimate part of his being, into his secrets. Yes, love in adoration touches the heart of our God: for him, nothing is more precious.

So true adoration which links us to Jesus is a love which must be lived. It is not a simple prayer, and certainly not a prayer muttered in passing or only concerned with oneself. True prayer, prayer which pleases God, turns our entire being towards him in a gesture of pure love, in an impulse of adoration. The prayer of adoration shows itself in a gesture, an impulse or an act which manifests our love to God and to our brothers and sisters. It is here that we find the root of charitable love, that true charity which takes us out of ourselves and into an encounter with God: then God himself carries us back to our brothers and sisters.

Meeting people is the essential prerequisite for knowing them, finding out about and appreciating them, developing a bond of friendship or love with them. It is the same with God. But meeting God is always a major event in someone's life, for God is not like everyone else: God is Love. Meeting him means meeting total Love, unconditional, overwhelming Love! This is what is drawing us.

Christ, in the Eucharist, is a living person who draws us to him: *And I, when I am lifted up from the earth, will draw all people to myself* (Jn12:32). Jesus is already accomplishing this for us in the Eucharist. Even if we cannot see him with our eyes of flesh, his living presence can be striking, showing us that he is there. This *I am*, which is Moses' name for God, is the name that Jesus gives himself to indicate that he is God: *Before Abraham was, I am* (Jn 8:58). This name which means eternal and ever-real presence is the name of Jesus-Eucharist: he is always there, present for us, in the midst of us, until the end of time.

If we want to meet him we have to make ourselves available and be present in his presence. That is what he expects of us. Adoration of the Eucharist requires that we approach his presence and remain there: we must spend time with him and only with him. We must dedicate enough time to enter into a state of silence and remain there. That is how we will develop the heart-to-heart encounter he wishes to draw us into. It is he who takes the initiative. Within a heart with no pretensions, a gentle and humble heart, he can do anything and everything. For out of this meeting, *he has scattered the proud in the thoughts of their hearts...and sent the rich away empty.* But *he has filled the hungry with good things* (cf. Lk 1:51-53). So did he fill Mary of Bethany, who came to him in humility, letting the grace of the forgiven sinner flow into her. She said nothing, but entered into adoration. She loves and adores her Living God too much to use words. That kind of love needs no words from mankind, created by God.

In true silence, the humble heart has nothing to say for itself, has nothing in it to give. It is a meek and apt vessel, simply drinking in grace until it is full. So God is the one who is speaking, just as in the episode of the perfumed ointment. Mary of Bethany says nothing. She comes forward silently and expresses the pure impulse of love which is driving her, by means of a gesture. Not a single word has passed her lips. She has loved with a spontaneous gesture.

Jesus is the one who speaks, but his words are not uttered as encouragement or thanks to the one who poured the perfume over him. There is no need for that. A heart-to-heart encounter has happened between Jesus and the woman. No words are necessary. The love in adoration which has overwhelmed her has allowed her to glimpse the heights and depths of Christ's love for her and for all sinners. In order to save them, he will give his life. She has grasped this through intuition, through grace, and through love.

When Jesus speaks, it is for the benefit of the others, for those who are criticising her. Judas is their spokesperson, the one at the front of the queue. He is present as one who watches in order to bring about someone's downfall. Pride, jealousy and love of money have already eaten into his heart. He is trying to separate this woman from Jesus, and he uses a subtle kind of treachery. He attempts to contrast the love in adoration shown by the woman towards Jesus with charitable love to be shown towards the poor. He tries to divide opinion through lies. He knows very well that what he is saying is false and this is not the least of his sins. There is nothing but corruption in his heart.

Jesus' sayings and teachings have included the fact that the two commandments, loving God and loving one's neighbour, amount to the same thing. But hatred has entered into Judas' heart: he no longer exists within the bounds of love. He can no longer tolerate anyone loving Jesus, and loving him as much as this. The false pretext he employs is the most subtle of all, suggesting that the woman lacks charity by failing to think about the poor. But it is his own heart which has left love behind. He tries to sow the seed of doubt and confusion, thinking he will thus be able to distance the woman from Jesus, reject her, and whip up opposition amongst the others so they can chase her away.

Jesus knows that Judas has already betrayed him in his heart. He knows that Judas, the son of perdition, is the one who will very soon commit the act of betrayal. But it will not be just yet, and Jesus prevents him from going any further. The prince of darkness is subtle, but the love of Jesus-Eucharist is infinitely more powerful. Jesus speaks up in order to explain the meaning of Mary's gesture, and nothing more needs to be added: the discussion is closed. What really matters is something altogether different: the perfume poured out anticipates Christ's burial, and the woman's gesture anticipates the Passion.

We should all reflect on these astounding words for all this happens just before the Last Supper, and highlights the tragic contrast between the infinite love of Christ and Judas' utter lack of love. Love of the Eucharist and the mystery of betrayal are connected. Judas, one of the closest to Jesus, has heard and seen everything.

The greatest drama ever will be played out in a few hours' time. Jesus is trying to prepare his apostles for it, as he has tried many times before. But at the same time, the words he pronounces: *for the day of my burial*, are directed at Judas who has already made all the arrangements to have Jesus arrested and killed. More than any of the other apostles, Judas is aware of the stage being set. He, the loveless, is the principal player in this drama concerning Jesus who is Love.

And soon the crowds, acting out of ignorance and superficial understanding – and this isn't the least of their sins, either – will side with the loveless by crying

'Crucify him, crucify him!' They act in their short-term interest, choosing the easy answer, for hatred separates, divides and kills. But when hatred kills love, resurrection follows: "The third day he rose again." [2]

Hatred only triumphs for a little while, and only seemingly. It cannot kill love because love has no limits and is eternal. Judas on the other hand, the son of perdition, dies in his hatred. Despairing and wracked with anguish, he kills himself. He has been so close to the one who is love that he suffers the greatest torture conceivable. This is damnation, which means 'separation'. Separating yourself from love is damning yourself, and walking voluntarily into hell.

The striking thing is that all this happened just before the Last Supper, leading us to draw two conclusions:

– The mystery of the Eucharist, as a sacrifice, is linked to the mystery of betrayal. The sacrifice came about through betrayal, that monumental combat between the greatest love and the devil who separates, who stands in the way and who, unable to tolerate love, entered into Judas' heart. Can we not see these two mysteries linked in each of the disciples' lives, and especially in the lives of those wanting above all to love the Eucharist?

– The celebration of the Last Supper starts with Mary of Bethany, as she kneels in love and adoration at Jesus' feet. Mary represents the entire human race waiting to be saved by Jesus and Jesus alone, through his sacrifice. The celebration of the Eucharist begins here. Even before the Passover meal occurs, Mary worships Jesus as Saviour: he is the one who has come to conquer death. She loves and adores his person. His living presence is precious to her, and she shows him so before the sacrifice takes place. She gives thanks with her love so full of infinite gratitude: it is a Eucharistic love, a love filled with thanksgiving.

The Eucharist assumes its full significance here, for it includes and recognises the vocation of the baptised, which is to love and adore. It cannot be confined simply to the moment of sacrifice. There could be neither sacrifice nor nourishment if there had not been both the person and the presence first, the two being always inseparable.

The Eucharist is not limited to the only meal consisting of sacrifice and nourishment. If there are no guests, the meal means nothing. We must not forget the guests: the meal cannot take place without them. The sacrificial supper, the nourishment, is given for all who have been invited. It is the same with Eucharistic adoration. When we love and adore Jesus-Eucharist, we are celebrating his living person and his presence.

To adore Jesus in the Eucharist is to love him,
giving thanks for his person,
for his presence,
in a pure impulse of love.

Eukaristos, in Greek, means 'thank you', and this is what Eucharistic love is, a love of thanks for the person of Christ in his Eucharist. It is a very special love which springs from the heart of mankind in pure gratitude and thanksgiving. We understand that love in adoration is clearly not a form of prayer, and still less a devotional activity. ***It is love to be lived in unceasing homage to Jesus***: in intimate union with him. We can live this love even in this earthly life. We are called to live it fully and eternally in the Kingdom, and should start preparing ourselves straightaway.

Looking

Adoring Jesus is looking at him lovingly

There is no better definition of either adoration or loving. There is no need to talk at length about adoration: just live it. Adoring the Living Jesus in the Eucharist is very simple, otherwise the Lord would not be sending out this call to lay people living in the everyday world.

Jesus is engraving this appeal deep in our hearts, written in letters of fire: *"Don't let a single day go by without looking at me."* [3]

In doing this, he wants to produce souls of adoration with a burning, passionate love, living in the everyday world, who will look at the living person of Christ in the Eucharist with nothing but pure love. The Lord wants to teach the souls of adoration how to accomplish this act which is so very simple, but, in the context of a human life, is of enormous intensity.

Let's make a comparison, since there is a profound resemblance between divine love and human love: *Let us make humankind in our image, according to our likeness* (Gen 1:26). When we love someone deeply, we love him or her because he or she is that person. We love him in spite of the faults we are aware of, for no human being is perfect: there is no rational explanation. Our love is stronger than any human imperfection, or even any fault, when we truly love. It goes much further. It is when we go beyond ourselves and our simple affections that human love enters into and provides us with a glimpse of that love which is divine.

When two beings love each other, they are drawn towards each other. They do not ask themselves how to love, or what love is: they have an interior understanding. They do not try to explain it, they just live it. When a mother loves her child, she does not analyse intellectually how she is going to love her child: she simply experiences her love. She will show it by taking care of her child, by giving up her time, her strength, everything she has, her whole life.

Loving: it is the simplest and the most precious thing in the world. It might seem to us that this precious thing is given rather a rough ride these days, and is stifled and disfigured. Do we still know what true love is? Do we still have the time to love, or is it becoming a luxury, something which is no longer acceptable because it is neither reliable nor guaranteed to bring in a return!

The Lord himself brings all these questions into focus in our lives, by drawing us into love in adoration. If human love is capable of going beyond all that is finite and imperfect, if it is capable of going beyond the suffering which we or others bring about, love in adoration will be more than capable of soaring up to rest in the divine, adorable person of Christ in the Eucharist.

Jesus, of course, has no faults. He is perfection itself, the infinite, eternal and permanent being. His love never falters. We, on the other hand, who are stained by original sin, we are always having our 'ups and downs'. Our love, our charity, that fire which lives inside us, is easily unsettled: it varies in intensity.

Jesus' love remains always strong and alive, drawing us to him unceasingly. How easy it is for us, at any moment and no matter what the circumstances, to turn our gaze of pure love towards Jesus, true God and true Man, actually present in the Eucharist. How solid, how concrete, such love is for us!

The more we fix our gaze on the living person of Jesus, the more will we be dazzled by the rays of his glory, and the more will he transform us and fill us with joy. He will give us that deep peace which transcends all trials and suffering, and leads us to the heart of God.

Total commitment

The gaze of adoration which draws us towards the person of Christ is only a response to God's loving gaze upon us. This response requires us to:

— make a total commitment which engages our whole life, making it clear that adoration and life are linked;
— be fully aware that God gazes upon us first.

It is a commitment of our entire being, made with heartfelt goodwill. The notion of goodwill itself implies the activation of the will, and since this will is goodwill, it means that it is concerned with a desire to do good; to give pleasure; to please God. If we have not yet discovered God, we are concerned with finding him. Such a desire is prompted by love.

Desire and love go together, work together. We have a desire for love. Goodwill is a desire for love in which desire and love are both present.

In the spiritual life, it is important that desire and love go hand-in-hand. If they are separated, they will soon become obsessive and distorted. Together, they remain in equilibrium.

This is the fundamental attitude of the person seeking God. In his desire to meet him, he wants to look at him in order to know him better and love him more. Desire, made up of goodwill, is necessary. This desire carries with it the commitment of the whole person, turning the gaze of adoration upon Jesus into a genuine commitment of his life. If we separate adoration from life, we will be living a lie.

Adoration is a commitment to live every moment of our lives with God's gaze resting upon us. Conversely, we cannot separate the commitments of our daily lives from the adoration due to God, because we are his children. Otherwise, our lives lose all their meaning. A life of adoration is therefore understood as an unconditional commitment, the deepest kind possible: it signifies a commitment to Christ, taken on during adoration and lived in a concrete sense in our daily actions and behaviour.

There is no need for regulations, charters, or those strings of obligations which sometimes weigh heavily upon us and can hinder the soul's impulse – *"You load people with burdens hard to bear"* (Lk 11:46), Jesus said to the Pharisees. A life of adoration exists above and beyond all these, and provides answers to many questions. There is no approved method, no recipe for success allowing automatic entrance into adoration.

The question people so often ask, "What do you do during adoration?" has no answer. Or at least, the answer would be too simplistic, because this isn't the right question. There is no set procedure to enter into adoration: adoration belongs to a different order. It is linked to *life*. It is a love to be lived, a love which sets you free.

It allows the soul to meet God without any intermediary or the presence of any other person. It is a heart-to-heart encounter, a direct, personal link from soul to soul.

And no one will take your joy from you (Jn 16:22). No one can take it over and control it or steal it from us. This is our true freedom as children of God, the freedom God wants for each one of us.

This life of adoration cannot be just one option which we choose along with various others, for it is even more than a personal commitment. It is a decision taken by love: it is a desire of love in which the entire being, body and soul, allows itself to be taken over by God. It is therefore God who is in control, for he is Master and Lord: he is Master of spiritual life and Master of all life.

And call no one your father on earth,
For you have one Father – the one in heaven.
Nor are you to be called instructors,
For you have one instructor, the Messiah.
(Mt 23:8-10)

This sort of childlike trust provides the answer to another range of problems, expressed as follows: "Since the prayer of adoration is carried out in silence, it leaves us feeling that we can't concentrate, or else that we're empty inside, with nothing to do, nothing to say ". In other words, we are bored and we do not know what to do with this silence or how to fill it. This would imply that silence before God is empty, void of meaning, and that our whole life is our own doing. We fill it with our own ideas, efforts, activities, plans and amusement. If this is the case, we are not in a state to receive anything from God. There is no room for him inside us, just like on Christmas Eve: "There was no room for him at the inn". The noise, the comings-and-goings and the crowds left no room for him. This is exactly how the world is.

It is the same with us: we recreate the night before Christmas. There is no room inside us for him. Like butterflies attracted by the artificial light which then kills them, many of us are attracted by all that is happening in the world. When nothing is happening, we feel completely lost.

Happy are they who, although living in the world, seek a place of silence, as did Mary and Joseph that Christmas night, knowing that silence is essential if we want to draw God into us, to meet him, see him… and adore him!

This place of silence, this interior space for God, is only found in simplicity, when all that is unnecessary is stripped away. It is often through such moments of interior poverty and deprivation that God draws us all the more to him and into him.

It is perhaps this which sometimes alarms and frightens us. Our first, very human reaction, is to turn away.

How sad this is, for we close the door to our own true happiness. If we want to cross this threshold of interior poverty without fear, we have to abandon ourselves entirely to God, to Divine Providence, placing all our trust in him, as a child trusts his Father completely.

This is the secret of a life of adoration: giving ourselves to God, giving up our will and thus allowing him to take all the initiatives. This is the way to let adoration and life go hand in hand. We cannot adore God without finding that something in our life has changed!

We can already see how much a life of adoration brings together our interior life, our sacramental life and our everyday behaviour, uniting them all. None of these can be separated from the others: an immensely strong cohesive force binds them together. When we understand this, find it and actually live it, a unique pathway to union with God opens up before us. And it is 'the way': *I am the Way*, Jesus tells us.

It seems to me that this Way is the way for the Church's future, the way of the third millennium and of the new evangelisation. It is founded on Christ, on our being attached to his person in adoration, and on our consequent conduct in everyday life which Jesus announces in the Gospel as being the source of greatest happiness: Blessed are the meek, the merciful, for the Kingdom of God is theirs! The Kingdom already in your midst!

God is gazing upon us

On this journey which calls upon all our goodwill, we are aware that we are being led and guided, and are only responding to a call we have heard, or to an attraction like that felt by someone who is thirsty and is groping around, searching for the spring which will quench that thirst. We are pulled along like a starving man who looks for the food which will save him, and without which he cannot live.

Thus is born the certainty that God's love is there first. God loved us first, St John tells us. He takes the initiative in everything. If we are aware of this and acknowledge it, we live in this love and allow ourselves to be guided and taught by him. If we apply this awareness to the gaze of adoration which pulls us towards Christ and causes us day after day to go further into the intimacy of his love, we cannot help but recognise that God's gaze is taking hold of us, entering into us, surrounding us.

From the start, God's gaze rested upon the world which he created, and his gaze brought life into being. From all eternity, God's gaze has rested upon each of us: *The Spirit of the Lord is upon me*, says Jesus in the synagogue at Nazareth (Lk 4:18). This gaze brings light into the deepest parts of our soul: *I am the light of the world*, Jesus tells us (Jn 8:12).

When we open ourselves up and become receptive to God's gaze falling on us, we are turning ourselves towards him, towards he who **is**. And it is all that we *are* which is being pulled towards him. Just as a plant grows naturally towards the light because it is vital for its survival, it is just as vital for us to turn our gaze towards God. This is quite simply a response to his gaze upon us. Within this wonderful exchange, God takes hold of us in order to draw us towards him. We feel an irresistible attraction for him, and when we are in a state of grace we allow ourselves to be led, to be won over by this gaze. The intimate presence of God is so strong that we feel it inside us. He lives inside us, setting up home here on earth inside us: we in him and he in us.

Sadly and all too often, we try to run away from God's gaze upon us, because of sin. We are wounded by sin. So we construct our own barriers, obstacles and defence mechanisms. We hide ourselves, like Adam and Eve after their act of disobedience, when they could no longer bear to feel God gazing upon them, sending a searchlight into the darkest corners of their hearts. Sin often stops us allowing ourselves to be brought into the light by God's gaze. But he who loves light comes to the light. He opens himself up to God's gaze and turns his face towards him. There is then a marvellous exchange, illustrated by this most beautiful line from the psalm:

Look to him, and be radiant.
(Ps 34:5)

But is it actually possible to look at God? The Hebrew people in the Old Testament couldn't: all they could see was the dense cloud. All the people turned towards it and adored it, feeling the presence of God very strongly. The dense cloud was full of light, and was the manifestation of the glory of God. Moses was the living proof of this as, coming down from the mountain where God had revealed himself, his face reflected the light of this glory so vividly that he had to conceal it behind a veil when he addressed the people.

Moses is a splendid example of the love in adoration to which God is calling souls of adoration at this dawn of the third millennium. In fact, God decreed this love in adoration to him in a single commandment, so he would engrave it forever on the tablets of stone:

You shall love the Lord your God
with all your heart, and with all your soul,
and with all your might.
Keep these words that I am commanding you today
in your heart
(Deut 6:5-6)

A major step forward was brought about however with the coming of Christ:

- for the Hebrew people in the desert, the tent of the Covenant was the place where everything happened, and the dense cloud above the tent was evidence of the presence of God;
- later, in Jerusalem, the presence of God was located in the Temple, where the Jews went to adore him;
- but for us, thanks to Christ, the centre of everything is his living presence, body and blood, in the Eucharist. And this is only a preparation, an introduction to the vision of glory, that face-to-face meeting to which we are all invited.

This is a marvellous development in which Jesus plays a central part, since it is through him that we will come face to face with God, will actually see his face. This is what the Incarnation has done for us. In Jesus, God makes himself **close** and **present** in a new way. Close and present: those two indispensable characteristics of love.

Mary and Joseph, the shepherds, the magi, then later the disciples, and so many others who followed Jesus, listened to him and saw him pass by them. All these really saw the face of God: *Whoever has seen me has seen the Father* (Jn 14:9).

So, God reveals his face to men through Christ. It is thanks to the Incarnation that we know the very face of God. And it is once again thanks to the Incarnation that we will be able to adore God unceasingly in the life of glory, through looking at the holy Face of Christ.

Christ gives us the face of God. We can now adore his features and imprint them deeper and deeper into ourselves, preparing for that meeting *when we will see him as he is* (1 Jn 3:2). Perhaps the Father gave us his Son so that we might adore his Holy Face unceasingly and eternally, and so that the Father might delight in us, seeing his Son's face reflected in us, transforming us all truly into more sons and daughters of the Father.

During the course of his public life, Jesus often lets his gaze rest upon someone. This is always an important moment: an encounter. But it is always Jesus who looks first. He is a step ahead of us. He leads the way in love. As Jesus said to Nathanael: *I saw you under the fig tree* (Jn 1:48).

When Jesus looks at someone, this person who has up to now been anonymous, becomes **somebody**: an individual, a character. This is what happens with Matthew, with Zacchaeus, with the Samaritan woman and with each of the disciples whom Jesus called to follow him. Their names are now written into the Gospel, right up to the end of time. The same thing happens to all the sick people Jesus healed, to all the sinners who changed their lives after simply meeting his gaze. And it is the same with each one of the billions of human beings on earth: the name of each one of us is written in heaven because Jesus the Christ, the one who saves, has set his gaze of power and tenderness upon each of us simultaneously, and all because of Love.

In this present stage in the history of the Church we cannot see Jesus walking along the roads of Palestine. We cannot yet see him directly in glory, like on Mount Tabor. But we can see him in the Eucharist: thanks to Christ, all is present in his living presence.

Adoration is letting our gaze rest upon him while we love him, and it is only a response to his gaze upon us. How can we claim to love and adore God unless we do so through Christ, who gave himself to us in the Eucharist as a pathway to the Father and to the glory which is waiting for us?

Jesus-Eucharist is waiting for us to look at him in adoration so that he can reveal the Father to us. Adoration draws us into the mystery of the love of the Trinity. But Christ is the way in.

> *Listen! I am standing at the door, knocking;*
> *if you hear my voice*
> *and open the door,*
> *I will come in to you and eat with you,*
> *and you with me.*
> (Rev 3:20)

This is God's plan for every soul, for every home which wants to open the door to his Love, welcome it in and be guided in all things by it.

Changing our lives

During love in adoration we rest our gaze upon the Living Jesus in the Eucharist and all of our being turns towards him. When our gaze turns to Jesus, our hearts and minds are drawn along in the same direction. A conversion takes place in the deepest parts of our being, allowing Christ to effect a transformation of our beings in him, until we are transfigured.

The hour is coming, Jesus told the Samaritan woman, *when the Father will be adored in spirit and in truth* (Jn 4:23-24). The important word here is 'truth', because the truth of our adoration is linked to the truth of our lives.

Conversion

This is what Jesus is referring to when he speaks to the Samaritan woman. He is leading her towards a major encounter, towards the recognition that he is the Messiah, the Son of the Living God. But the truth implicit in that encounter, during which there is undoubtedly an act of adoration on the part of the woman, also involves a radical change in the woman.

This change involves **the conversion of her heart,** from now on turned towards God and fixed upon him; and a changing of her life immediately afterwards. The Samaritan saw Christ and from that moment on her life would remain in that light. She would abandon false happiness for the only true happiness, for she had found the all-inclusive meaning of her life. Her heart was filled to the brim. Jesus had allowed her to look upon him with a gaze of adoration: she had thus caught a glimpse of his divinity. For when the Samaritan saw Jesus exhausted by the side of the well, she saw his human nature. How could she guess that she was standing right next to the divine person, the second person of the Blessed Trinity, the Son of God himself, the Messiah awaited for so long... And yet she met him!

The true gaze of adoration allowed the divinity of Christ in his humanity to be glimpsed. In fact, the divinity of Christ cannot be adored without his humanity, in other words, if his humanity is forgotten. Love in adoration is distinguished precisely by the delicate accomplishment of loving and adoring Christ at one and the same time in his human and in his divine nature.

True adoration thus cannot be reduced to a ritual. It cannot be merely an exterior devotion in God's honour: never just a matter of formality. It involves the engagement of all our being, and along with the engagement of all our being goes the truth of our lives. "It is not enough to say we are Christians, we must be Christians", says John Paul II. True adoration changes our hearts. A change takes place gently and little by little within us, sometimes even without our knowledge. There is a conversion which purifies, and then transformation. Even if the initial encounter happens suddenly, conversion is a path which continues for the rest of our lives. A purification is necessary, leading to a transformation.

In the presence of the Living God, the heart opens up to his light, to his mercy. Realising that it is poor, weak and utterly destitute, it becomes humble and turns towards God. It calls to God. It feels the need for God – an absolute need – in order to be saved.

Throughout the entire history of salvation, the conversion factor has remained essential and constant. It is an attitude founded on the profound sense of truth which mankind must feel towards God, towards our living and moving God, and an attitude which we find is still necessary in order to receive grace. We have to let God act through us. The requirement to be truthful, honest and pure is repeated in the words of all the prophets of the Old Testament, inspired by the Holy Spirit, the Spirit of God. They warn endlessly about attitudes which are nothing but superficial, and against deceit through the kind of worship which is concerned only with ceremonial. What they care about is always a true relationship with God. They proclaim the absolute priority of establishing a *personal, living and true* relationship with the Living God whom we must know and love with a true love. These ideas are wonderfully expressed by Hosea, Amos, Isaiah and Ezekiel:

> *For thus says the Lord to the house of Israel:*
> *Seek me and live.*
> (Am 5:4)

> *It is not sacrifice which pleases me,*
> *but the contrite and humble heart.*
> (Mic 6:6-8)

And sometimes, God even expresses grief! Oh, the grief of God:

> How far their hearts are from me!

We discover – through all these calls from God, and in order to establish a true relationship with him – the need for a humble, unassuming and submissive heart:

> *Seek the Lord, all you humble of the land,*
> *who do his commands;*
> *seek righteousness, seek humility;*
> (Zeph 2:3)

God can do nothing with 'proud' hearts, that is hearts which are haughty and arrogant:

> *He has scattered the proud in the thoughts of*
> *their hearts.*
> *He has brought down the powerful from*
> *their thrones,*
> *and lifted up the lowly.*
> (Lk 1:51-52)

sings the Virgin Mary in her *Magnificat*.

The broken heart of the Old Testament, that is the contrite, repentant and humble heart, is one which is already turning towards God, ready to meet him if it has not already done so. This is the essential requirement for a true relationship with God.

We realise this when, immediately preceding the coming of the Messiah, John the Baptist suggests baptism by water as a means of achieving a profound conversion of the heart. This baptism involved repentance for sins as part of a desire for forgiveness and purification, and also required the changing of one's life.

This was a true preparation which pleased God, for the people's hearts were really preparing themselves to welcome his Son. They were preparing themselves for his coming, in that spirit of conversion which is so pleasing to God. And John the Baptist called upon them to change their lives:

Whoever has two coats must share with anyone
who has none;
And whoever has food must do likewise.
(Lk 3:11)

Do not extort money from anyone
by threats or false accusation,
and be satisfied with your wages.
(Lk 3:14)

These were constant reminders of the need to integrate the quest for the Living God as exemplified by the practices of the day – rituals, devotions, sacrifices – with a truly heartfelt desire, which alone can bring about a change in our attitudes and our lives. One without the other is, in the eyes of God, a mere piece of trickery which he abhors and rejects:

For I will leave in the midst of you
a people humble and lowly.

> *They shall seek refuge in the name of the Lord –*
> *the remnant of Israel;*
> *they shall do no wrong*
> *and utter no lies,*
> *nor shall a deceitful tongue*
> *be found in their mouths.*
> *Then they will pasture and lie down,*
> *and no one shall make them afraid.*
> (Zeph 3:12-13)

If such appeals have been made throughout the Old Testament, while the coming of the Messiah was awaited, how much more urgent and pressing they become with the arrival of Christ. For God's wishes are the same today, but expressed now by the Son of God himself, the Word sent to speak to us. With the coming of Christ, there has been a major step forward in the relationship of trust between each one of us and God. There is a presence and a closeness which were not made manifest before the coming of Christ.

In the Gospel, Jesus is not only forever seeking genuine commitment from everyone he meets, but is asking for more: for that trust which leads to true faith, a commitment of faith in his person. He often asks the question:

> *Do you believe in the Son of Man?*
> (Jn 9:35)

and states:

> *Did I not tell you that if you believed,*
> *you would see the glory of God?*
> (Jn 11:40)

Before each healing or conversion, Jesus asks for an act of faith:

Your faith has saved you.
(Lk 18:42)

In the same vein, the act of faith recognising Jesus as the Son of God involves or implies changing one's life:

Go your way, and from now on do not sin again.
(Jn 8:11)

What a delicate touch Jesus' love has! He makes no reproaches, but leads each one to see for himself what is disordered in his life, what needs to be changed: *Go, call your husband* (Jn 4:16) he says to the Samaritan woman.

He doesn't lay down conditions. But each person who has met Christ and received his love goes away with his heart on fire. Each one, acting out of a sense of the vast freedom within them, becomes personally concerned with the urgent need to change or improve anything which fails to match up to such love! We can see this in Zacchaeus and so many others. The changes they make to their lives show their commitment to the person of Christ: but it is this commitment which comes first and which determines all the rest.

Yes, Jesus is truly the master of the spiritual life, and quite simply the only Master of life. For once he takes hold of our lives, he directs the whole of our lives himself. In order to show us what he expects from us, Jesus gives us an example by presenting us with little children. He is waiting for us to come to him with childlike hearts:

Unless you change and become like children, you will never enter the kingdom of heaven.
(Mt 18:3)

Or again, there is that moment of resonating joy when this prayer springs from Jesus' lips:

> *I thank you, Father,*
> *Lord of heaven and earth,*
> *because you have hidden these things*
> *from the wise and the intelligent*
> *and have revealed them to infants.*
> (Lk 10:21)

Christ's mercy is there, right on our doorstep! Jesus is waiting: we only have to reach out! He has placed within our reach the means for achieving holiness, for the example he gives us seems almost easy.

There is actually the most marvellous, gentle sense of innocence in a young child, and we are drawn towards it. It is the mark of infancy, which knows neither deceit nor trickery. The young child's heart is not divided: the child is not a *whited sepulchre*, that term used by Jesus as a terrible reproach to certain people. The young child is true. The way he behaves and the way he feels inside are one, and Jesus wants to bring us back into this same dimension of truth. The child's heart is unassuming, pure and humble, matching the requirements for holiness outlined by Jesus on the mountain. This is where we find truth in our daily lives: in hearts which are unassuming, pure and humble.

But there is still much more: by giving us little children as an example, Jesus wants to tell us that from now on the relationship between mankind and God has entered a new stage, and can be richer and deeper. With our hearts turned towards God and changes made to our lives, Jesus calls upon us to develop a *filial* attitude towards God who is the Father.

Transformation

The profoundly trusting relationship which characterises a little child's attitude towards its father must now be adopted by us in our attitude towards God. In other words, this must be the attitude of all of God's children towards their heavenly Father. Jesus' coming actually reveals to us *his Father*, who is also *our Father*.

This represents a radical change in the entirety of our interior life. We might say that Jesus' coming has changed all the rules of the game. Jesus wants to take us up onto a different level, one which we had never glimpsed before, and which is way out of our own reach.

Jesus, the Son, brings us with him into a completely new relationship with the Father. Thanks to Christ, we too are sons and daughters of God, and we can behave as such. There is no fear, no separation, no barrier between mankind and God: we, with Christ, are children of the Father. Our relationship with God can no longer be reduced to legalistic or formal requirements, and we can no longer cower before him. Through grace we never even dreamed of, our souls may now leap towards God, as a little child, full of trust, leaps towards its father. This is the new conversion open to us. The change brought about is so radical that it effects a real **transformation** in us. We are not only turning towards God in conversion, but the conversion itself becomes turned into a transformation: we have changed our state of being. We were slaves, and we have become not only friends, but far more: we have become sons and daughters.

The quotation from Matthew 18:3 has such a vast significance that we need to let the words re-echo in our hearts like a silent but immensely powerful prayer!

This attitude of filial trust is simple and holds nothing back, and it is this which Jesus calls for in his public life each time he heals, delivers, comforts or gives hope or life: he asks for a total commitment of trust. This commitment is nothing other than an act of faith. Faith in what? In a better life, in possessions, riches, better health? No, faith in **Someone!** For those who come to him with hidden motives of self-interest go away again empty-handed.

But who do you say that I am?
You are the Messiah, the Son of the living God.
(Mt 16:15)

With trust like that, Jesus can do anything. He can heal, bring back to life, free people from their sins, and give everlasting life. He can also entrust someone with a mission:

You are Peter...
(Mt 16:18)

Go therefore and make disciples of all nations, baptising them in the name of the Father and of the Son and of the Holy Spirit.
(Mt 28:19)

Go into all the world and proclaim the good news to the whole creation.
(Mk 16:15)

But commitment means much more than this. The question Jesus put was not just, do you believe? but, do you love me?

Faith and love go together when there is genuine trust. Only Christ can ensure that we are given a childlike heart full of trust. All the graces which are obtained on our behalf come from the Cross of Christ: they pour out in cascades from his open Heart on the cross, from his body given up and from his blood spilled for us. This is how he won for us the privilege of being children of the Father.

How can we obtain this trusting, childlike heart today? It is in the Eucharist that Jesus offers us unceasingly his body given up, his blood that was shed. Always there for us in the Blessed Sacrament, Jesus reshapes us in his own image when we adore him and especially when we adore him visibly there before our very eyes.

Utterly humble in the Eucharist, Jesus teaches us just how far he went in his total trust of the Father. He abandoned himself into his Father's hands:

> *Father, if you are willing,*
> *remove this cup from me;*
> *yet, not my will but yours be done.*
> (Lk 22:42)

Jesus humbled himself in every respect, abandoned himself to the will of his Father, *to the point of death – even death on a cross* (Phil 2:8). He submitted his own will to that of his Father, so that their two wills matched perfectly, making only one:

> *As you, Father, are in me*
> *and I am in you.*
> (Jn 17:21)

In adoration of his body and his blood, Jesus wants to teach us how to abandon our wills. This means giving up our ideas and our own individual points of view in order to shape ourselves more and more in accordance with the will of the Father. This is the real sacrifice, the real 'breaking of the heart'. We know that it is difficult. It's completely impossible if our human nature is left to its own devices.

But Jesus has the **divine power** to **transform us within himself** so that we too may become sons and daughters of the Father with him, the Son.

Jesus established the Eucharist in accordance with the will of the Father, so that he would be everything for everyone. Consecrating ourselves to the Living Person of Christ, however, as we do in the Houses of Adoration, means striving endlessly to become '*eucharised*', to become like Jesus who gives himself to us in the Eucharist. *Being eucharised also involves abandoning our own will in favour of that of the Father.* This is why the consecration to the Living Jesus in the Eucharist, as encouraged by the Houses of Adoration, is an act of self-abandon.[4]

Although impossible, once again, for our human nature, such an act of abandon is possible through pure grace. It is possible through the special grace springing from the pierced Heart, from the Eucharistic body of Jesus given up for us, from his blood which was shed in order to obey the Father in all things.

Reshaping our own will to that of God, little by little, means we have to undergo many trials, much interior purification and a sense of progressive detachment: this cannot happen without a certain amount of suffering.

When Jesus compares us, as children of God, to the branches of a vine, he is warning us of what is in store for us:

I am the true vine,
and my Father is the vinegrower.
(Jn 15:1)

We have to let the Father cut, prune and trim so that the branches will bear fruit. In the same way, we should let the Father cut and prune, snipping off all that is evil in us, of course, but also all that is imperfect, all that serves no purpose, and all that makes us waste our time, turning us away or separating us from God.

But what is the point of this turning of the heart, this conversion, and then this transformation which God brings about in us? What is God aiming at, if we can put it like that? God is seeking hearts. In his untiring love for mankind, God is always trying to attach us to him, as the branch is attached to the vine, so that we will be an integral part of his vine. What God wants, what he longs for, is to take hold of us: *The Lord took me from following the flock,* says the prophet Amos when he is questioned (Am 7:15).

Ever since the coming of Christ, our attachment to the Living God is via the person of the Son of God made man.

God does not transform us through pruning, cutting and trimming because he wants to make us suffer. He does it in order to attach us to himself in the person of his Son Jesus, to make us resemble as much as possible this only and perfect Son who is offered in the Eucharist. "I want to let myself be led in all things, letting myself be shaped and modelled by the hands of Divine Providence."[5]

It hurts when we let ourselves be shaped and modelled, but it is the only way to become *eucharised*. Once we are free, purified and detached, we will be able to turn towards God with our whole being. What God wants is for our hearts to look towards him: he wants us to yearn for the gaze of our soul to rest upon Jesus-Eucharist so we can tell him that we love him and adore him. We want to surrender our trusting, childlike heart in total abandon so that he can take full hold of it. And when Christ takes hold of us, he does so in order to REIGN within us. When Jesus reigns in a heart, he transforms it: "I want to reign in every heart."[6]

Transfiguration

With the coming of Christ, the conversion referred to in the Old Testament thus becomes outdated. It is no longer enough. Jesus leads us into a relationship which is totally trusting towards him, and towards his Father who is also our Father; it is altogether one of a son or daughter. We are able to understand this because we know that Jesus even gives us his life so that we may become sons and daughters of God, and in order to obtain salvation for us.

In giving himself to us, body surrendered and blood shed, Jesus is not satisfied with converting us: he **saves** us. There is an enormous difference. We achieve a change of state, a transformation. But even this transformation is only another step, leading us to transfiguration.

Baptism by water becomes baptism in the blood of Christ. Because of this, the Eucharist is a central, deciding factor in our personal lives and in the life of the entire Church. It is certainly the blood of Christ which from now on purifies us, but what is far more important, it saves us. St John tells us: *The blood of Jesus his Son cleanses us from all sin* (1 Jn 1:7) and St Paul says: *In him we have redemption through his blood* (Eph 1:7).

The blood of Christ purifies us through the sacraments and in adoration. This purification is not just the constantly-needed conversion: it is the restoring of our entire being, which becomes a new creature: *See, I am making all things new*, says the Lord (Rev 21:5). *A new heaven and a new earth* (Rev 21:1).

Baptised in the death and Resurrection of Christ, we are transformed and we will be resurrected with him until, one day, we will be **transfigured**. Because of Christ and through Christ, conversion here on earth can now lead to transformation. *Transformation will in turn lead to transfiguration, once he has appeared in glory.*

We are waiting in hope for transfiguration, and this will happen when we enter through Christ into that glory which is his. It is Christ who will bring about this passage into transfiguration. Yes, Christ is our Passover, in other words our passage, the only passage which takes us:

> ***from the conversion of the Old Testament***
> ***to transformation through the Eucharist;***
> ***from Eucharistic transformation***
> ***to transfiguration in glory.***

This process of radical change is already underway, but it will not be completed until we are fully present in the Kingdom, when through Christ, we will be fully introduced into the mystery of the love of the Trinity. For the moment, we are still on the road and the transformation is taking place in us throughout our lives, day after day, thanks to the Bread of Life and the Source of Life which we receive during each Eucharist and during each time of adoration.

Receiving the body and blood of Christ takes on a significance of infinite dimension when we prepare ourselves in the silence of adoration. Receiving the body and blood of Christ bears unimagined fruits when, rather than coming to an end, the Eucharist is prolonged in a thanksgiving which is profound, loving and adoring.

We could say that a life of adoration is an essential and integral part of the Eucharist, preparing for it and prolonging it, letting Christ remain present and active within us.

We are thus led progressively, day by day, from this visible world *to a new heaven and a new earth.*

Through the blood of Christ, we are already drinking the *new wine* of the Kingdom he is telling us about.

> ***From conversion to transformation***
> ***we are called,***
> ***because of Christ,***
> ***to be transfigured.***
> ***Yes, indeed, look to him and be radiant.***

NOTES

1. Psalm 34:5.
2. Apostles' Creed.
3. Angot, Marie-Benoîte, *Les Maisons d'adoration* (Fayard, 1995) p. 121.
4. *Les Maisons d'adoration,* p. 116.
5. *Les Maisons d'adoration,* p. 115.
6. Angot, Marie-Benoîte, *Le Mystère de l'Amour vivant* (Fayard, 1994) p. 175.

2
The life within us

*"A living water is murmuring within me:
'Come to the Father!'"*[1]

Adoration and the interior life

The life of adoration which we have begun to examine is a pathway for conversion leading, via Christ, to transformation. Adoration of the body and blood of Christ develops our interior being. Sweeping aside the superficial, which only distracts our attention, it leads us into the living depths of ourselves, where God is waiting for us so he can demonstrate his presence to us in profound silence.

Experience shows us that love of the Eucharist develops and strengthens our interior life, as opposed to the life concerned only with appearances. The development of our inner life gives rise to an ever-increasing desire to let it take over completely.

*And should by chance you not know
where to find Me,
do not go here and there;
but if you wish to find Me,
in yourself seek Me.
Outside yourself seek Me not,
to find Me it will be
enough only to call Me,
then quickly will I come,
and in yourself seek Me.*[2]

This beautiful poem conveys a very deep truth, and one which St Theresa had experienced for herself. Like all the saints, she had found out how to find the **essential truth** in silence and in prayer:

- the essential truth, which is the at the very depths of our being, the interior life;
- the interior life which only exists in us because it is nurtured by the Holy Spirit.

But what do we mean by 'interior life'? To clarify this, let's think of those who are most dear to us. Do we *really* know them? Do we sometimes find that there are hidden aspects of their personalities, areas where we are not allowed in? The part of them which is their deepest self, their real personality, still slips away from us to a greater or lesser extent.

In the same way, each one of us can feel a chasm inside, and sometimes an enormous chasm, separating us from what other people know and say about us. It is an interior domain which is different to the outward appearance.

So we find that we have a vital decision to make in life: we can live our lives for the sake of 'appearances', in other words for outward show. Or we can do the opposite: we can choose to live in accordance with that which is of the most profound significance within us, delving into our deepest, most vital, selves.

If we live for the sake of appearances, our behaviour is intended to attract attention and to bring us praise and admiration, even if only within a small circle. We are forever performing in the gaze of others, as if we were in front of a mirror. We only do or say those things which others will approve of. We are really turning our lives into a long masquerade in which each person keeps a careful check on the mask he presents to others. But this apparently undemanding and agreeable piece of playacting leaves a huge void within the heart of the players, and a deep sense of dissatisfaction. We soon begin to feel like strangers, not just to others but to ourselves, which is even worse.

On the other hand, those of us who dare to be ourselves, to make decisions and to behave according to our own personal understanding of the truth no matter what the circumstances or the prevailing opinion, such people find that little by little an inner being is taking shape within them: a being who is wholehearted, solid and constant, a true heart of gold more precious than anything we can buy in the marketplace. This being is our very selves, our very 'substance' which no-one can take away from us, and at the same time we feel in harmony with what is best in other people.

We are now arriving at an understanding of what we call the ***interior life*** in its real sense. If we want to know what it is, we need to learn to look inside ourselves: we will see it flowing steadily behind all our thoughts and actions, like the sap rising steadily in the trunk of a tree, hidden by its bark. It is shaped by our most intimate thoughts:

- love which is generous and discreet
- respect for truth and Church teachings
- humility and freedom from material attachment
- steadfast courage
- interior joy.

On the other hand, this inner life force can be corrupted immediately by:

- lies
- deceit
- laziness
- vanity
- giving ourselves up to idle pleasures
- and worrying about what other people will say.

The interior life draws its being from our most intimate self, and feeds our thoughts and our actions through secret passageways like the arteries which take the blood to all the limbs of our bodies.

There is an interior life, developed to a greater or lesser extent, in each of us. We can no more do without it than we can do without our heartbeat. But we are often so completely taken over by our activities and by the world around us that we forget how to listen to what is happening inside us.

Even though some people accept the idea of the importance of an interior and personal life, it has to be said that life today, with all its noise and pressure, hardly encourages us to spend time developing it.

Looking at just one side of this question, we can define the society in which we live as a society based on images. Daily life and the world around us are increasingly represented to us by means of images.

But life – the life of each one of us – if we know how to look at it, contains something richer than all the films or novels in the world. It is hidden within us, but is our chief treasure. What waste and deprivation we inflict on ourselves if we confuse it with a series of images. Or if, spreading ourselves too thinly, we're so busy with the hustle and bustle of life that there is no room for it! But this is the danger which is lying in wait for us. If we don't take care, we will end up neglecting the interior life and it will slowly fade away, starved of nourishment. We will be draining off our inner 'substance' without even being aware of it.

We are aware, however, that everything which is founded on mere human values, based on the order of the natural world, is vulnerable and subject to change.

And then there is that event which none of us can escape: death. The death of our loved ones affects us deeply, but our own death will also come about.

So the same question arises again: is there something or rather someone within us who will live on unchanged despite all these changes and all these events? Is there an eternal something or someone who will survive beyond our death? Even beyond this great journey of death, our being lives on and maintains our existence, in the form of the most intimate part of ourselves.

We know, through our faith, that an Eternal Being holds us and supports us throughout all the changes affecting us, beyond life and death. He even reveals his name to us:

I am.
(Jn 8:58)

Being the Supreme Being, he gives to each of us a little of his everlasting being: he creates us in his own image and gives us an immortal spirit.

The response to our doubts and uncertainties, to our anxiety and our fundamental fragility is thus a response based on faith, and relies upon the words of God in the Scriptures. Jesus himself ends one of his teachings by saying: *Very truly, I tell you, before Abraham was, I am* (Jn 8:58).

Our God, who reveals himself in Jesus, is thus he

who rests firmly within us. This is easier to understand if we remember that the word 'substance' comes from two Latin words which mean 'stand' and 'beneath'. Substance is therefore that which remains underneath that which changes: that which remains eternally solid and unchangeable, but is hidden beneath appearances, invisible to human eyes.

The interior life cannot thus be limited to intellectual activity or moral concerns, however praiseworthy they might be. The interior life is the spiritual life, the life that never ends. It is the true life because it is affected neither by failure nor by death. The spiritual life, as its name suggests, is the life of the Spirit (the Holy Spirit) in us: the divine life which never ceases to whisper inside us. Our interior life becomes clear in the light of a new day, through faith which comes to the rescue of understanding. This 'interior region' which goes beyond the soul and is where God resides, is clearly alluded to in the following extract:

> Man is a being thirsting after eternity, even if he does not know what to call this profound desire burning within his heart. The cares of the times, and the impact of disordered passions, can pile up over and dim the interior eye made for the contemplation of infinity. Trapped within his hardened and closed circle, man can forget for a while his native destiny and his end.
>
> But, pulling back for brief moments from the blinding waves of distraction which keep him in chains on the outside, his inner self awakes and, feeling ill at ease, moves further inward. It journeys to the centre of his being, beyond his soul: to that region which is ***the dwelling place of his God***.

In the words of St Augustine:

> You made us for yourself and our hearts find no peace until they rest in you.[3]

> ...you were deeper than my inmost understanding... You were within me, and I was in the world outside myself... You were with me, but I was not with you.[4]

So God holds each of us like a precious treasure in the palm of his hand. He holds us and supports us, more accurately, in the depths of his heart. He places his life within us like a little grain or a spark of his own life, and, through Christ his Son, causes his blood to flow within the outer covering which is our body. And when, at the time of our death, we leave behind this covering, God will still preserve our hidden life until the time when he finally clothes it with the glorious body which is the only eternal home worthy of his presence.

God doesn't sustain us by remaining outside us, as is the case when our fellow men give us support. He touches us in the deepest parts of ourselves, arousing in us a life force we could never have imagined. Did Jesus not say to Martha:

> *I am the resurrection and the life.*
> *Those who believe in me,*
> *even though they die, will live.*
> (Jn 11:25)

This amazing fact is incomprehensible to mankind, but it reveals the immensity of life which is hidden in God. We know through our faith that God endows us with the essence of his life through the sacrament of baptism. From that moment on, the Trinity lives in us. But we also know that the battle is not over. It is very easy for us to allow this spark of the life of the Trinity inside us to fade away, through indifference or through successive refusals to acknowledge its presence.

In contrast, we know that God in his great bounty has put at our disposition all that is necessary for the soul to develop and strengthen his divine life in us. The graces given out through the sacraments are so many interior pathways made available to mankind so that we can come close to God. These interior pathways may be compared with the channels through which the sap circulates inside a tree. The scene described below can help us to grasp the analogy between the life of a child of God which develops in us from baptism onwards, and the living presence of Jesus in the Host:

> We are in an immense plain, and there is a magnificent tree. The most striking thing about it at first is its trunk: wide, huge, solid and reassuring. We cannot see the roots, of course, since they are underground, but we can guess that they are enormous, digging very deep in the soil to find all the nutrients necessary for the life of this majestic tree. The tree has a very thick and gnarled bark which has stood up to the test of wind, storm, heat and cold.
>
> Lifting up our eyes, we can see a dense network of branches laden with greenery. The tree must be healthy to bear so many leaves. And it has white flowers, countless numbers of exquisite little flowers, light and delicate. The boughs are so laden that they bend down gracefully to the ground, sprouting in turn more roots to make more trees.

How is that this tree is flourishing so much? If we could see inside the bark, we would see the rich, abundant sap rising. The sap provides excellent nourishment to the whole tree, making it more beautiful, making it flourish and bloom, ready to produce its life-bearing fruit.

The bark of the tree is only an envelope, like the covering of our body. The sap is the life of the Trinity flowing within us, bringing nourishment to our faculties. The tree cannot flower unless there is first of all a rich sap inside its trunk.

If the tree's trunk is gnawed away by rodents and invaded by parasites, the sap will be lost and the tree will die. But if we allow the life of the Trinity to circulate within us, like the sap of a tree, we will be surprised by the marvellous blooms we produce: purity, humility and mercy. And these blooms will sow their virtues in the soil (that is, in other souls) because virtue is contagious.

There is a certain resemblance between the life of the Trinity placed inside our body, as if in an envelope or inside some bark, and the real life of Jesus in the Host. Jesus really exists in what looks like bread. The Holy Trinity really lives inside us, inside this visible covering which is our body. The distinction between appearance and substance in the context of the Eucharist is also a relevant distinction in the reality of our lives.

It seems therefore that our human lives and our spiritual lives are very closely linked with the life of Jesus in the Host. There is a striking resemblance between the exterior appearance which is the envelope or covering, visible to our senses, and the substance, that is the living reality which is its solid, unchanging and eternal foundation.

In instituting the Eucharist, Jesus wanted to live among us and in our likeness until the end of time. Jesus takes humility so far as to want to live in our likeness. In the earthly paradise, God created Man in his own image. But in his Son who has come to save us, he makes himself identical to Man in every respect except sin, so that we will agree to be saved.

If only we could reflect more often on the fact that we resemble Jesus-Host! Our frail human forms are not much to boast about but we carry inside us a priceless treasure: we carry the life of Jesus inside us.

Our interior life is a living reality, just as the life of Jesus in the Host is a living reality. It can only develop if we have a great love for Jesus-Host, a great desire to receive him often and to adore him when he is really present within us. We cannot take Communion lightly. And we should always make the very most of those precious and sacred moments which follow Holy Communion.

The Christian life is thus first and foremost an interior life, because it finds its source in the interior life shaped in us by the Holy Spirit, the Spirit of Jesus. It draws its strength, its consistency and its solidity from the body and blood of Jesus. It develops when it invites him to occupy all the inner space of the soul during adoration. This is where the 'fruits of the Spirit', as St Paul called them, make themselves ready, like fruit slowly and secretly growing in the depths of the soil.

Those who love me will keep my word,
and my Father will love them,
and we will come to them and make our home
with them.
(Jn 14:23)

So let each one of us desire to be a 'home' for God, a place which God loves to make his home in, as Jesus makes his home in the Host. We can then carry him around everywhere with us, giving him to the world which has not yet received him.

The most important issue facing the Church today, and facing the society in which we live as well as each individual family, is the rediscovery of the most fundamental part of mankind. It is the rediscovery of the *interior life* shaped by these impulses of the spirit and of the heart, which are worth more than all the consumer goods in the world. The names we give to these impulses are: generosity, love of truth, desire for justice, interior freedom and above all, desire for God and for that which comes from the Spirit.

The greatest service which Christians can provide to mankind today is to bear witness to the reality and richness of such a life. We are all asked to provide this service: each one of us, each soul in adoration, and each House of Adoration which has adopted this mission as a vocation. Let's hope we can all respond to this request with all our hearts!

Adoration and the Evangelical Life

The Eucharistic life – and its immediate consequence, the interior life – lead and encourage us to put the values of the Gospel into practice.

> *Either make the tree good, and its fruit good;*
> *or make the tree bad, and its fruit bad;*
> *for the tree is known by its fruit.*
> Mt 12:33)

To come back to the example of the tree, certain conditions are needed if it is to flourish and grow: good soil, suitable weather conditions. But lots of work needs to be done as well: digging over the soil in the right season, pruning, watering, and spraying to stop it being attacked by insects or disease.

It is the same with us. The divine life is given to us in baptism, and this life will grow and become strong if we tend it and develop it by means of prayer and the sacraments, and in adoration. But that's not all. We must also, at the same time, engage in a *spiritual battle*. We must fight this battle against ourselves, against sin and against the inclination towards death which has been in us ever since the original sin. Baptism has of course made us children of God: this is essential. This first seed had to be sown in our soul, but it doesn't do everything for us. It isn't unfortunately a magic wand which effects an instant transformation. Our psychology, our inclinations and our instincts are still there: if we are to behave like children of God we must lead a new kind of life.

We have all that we need because Jesus himself during his public life gave us a code of values summing up the whole of the Gospel, and containing all the power of his teaching. This is the proclamation of promised happiness ringing out from the mountain top in the form of an unforgettable appeal to one and all: *Blessed*, Jesus tells us, *blessed are the poor in spirit, blessed are those who mourn, blessed are the meek* (Mt 5:3-11).

God has placed in the heart of each person, as a primary impulse, the desire for happiness. He wants to respond to this desire by sharing his own happiness with us, if we will let ourselves be led by him along the pathways he has prepared and points out to us.

Our God doesn't like unhappiness and takes no pleasure in scenarios of terror, despite the devil's attempts, by stirring up the anxieties and fears lurking deep inside us, to make us think he does. God always has happiness and joy in mind: he would like us to believe in them too, because of him.

This does not mean that a life of ease and comfort is promised us. In fact, the promises of the Gospel turn many of our ideas about happiness upside down. But they do guarantee that life's road leads us towards God's own happiness, whatever the difficulties we might meet, if we are able to travel on in faith and hope. All of God's promises take faith as their starting point.

Each time that God promises something, he asks us to have faith in his promise: faith which goes all the way. So Abraham had to keep going, believing faithfully in the promise he had received, even though it was not realised in his lifetime. It was the same for Moses. Not so long ago we find the example of the purest and most perfect faith in the divine promise: that of the Virgin Mary. Mary believed, in the face of and despite all outside appearances which indicated the opposite, those appearances which we spoke of earlier and which are only superficial elements. What happens on an interior level is something else altogether.

Blessed are you, cries Elizabeth on seeing Mary!

> *And blessed is she who believed*
> *that there would be a fulfilment of what*
> *was spoken to her by the Lord.*
> (Lk 1:45)

And we see the same promise of happiness proclaimed

this time by Jesus, a promise which is addressed to all who wish to follow Mary's example. *Blessed is the womb that bore you and the breasts that nursed you!* shouted a woman in the crowd. But Jesus replied:

> *Blessed rather are those who hear*
> *the Word of God and obey it!*
> (Lk 11:27-28)

To hear the Word of God is to receive it, believe in it, have faith in it. *To obey the Word of God* is to live it, to put it into practice. These two stages are of equal importance and are inextricably linked.

Jesus is evidently speaking of his mother here, and suggesting that everyone who is sincere in his love for God models himself upon her. He is telling us how we should behave if we wish to receive all the Gospel promises and, in a wider sense, to receive every Word which comes out of the mouth of God.

Listening to the Word of God

Listening is not simply a question of lending our ears, nor simply of hearing. We can hear something while we are distracted and in a hurry, like someone who is too busy, and then quickly forgets. We dispose of something we have heard superficially, just as we dispose of a useless object or one which gets in our way. How many times have we behaved in this way, even towards the Word of God when we have not really been paying attention, during Mass or elsewhere. The Word of God is not a set of ideals or just any old reading matter. It's life, it's even a living person: **The Word of God is the Word made flesh!**

Mary received the Word of God so well that the Word took on her flesh! How totally perfect Mary is! Mary believed with all her heart. She had faith in the Word and remained totally committed.

To listen is to welcome something into our lives and make it our own. If we keep in mind the fact that the living Jesus himself, the Word of God, is present in the Word of the Bible, we will be able to listen to it and welcome it as if we were at that very moment welcoming Jesus himself in person into ourselves and into our homes!

The living Jesus is present beneath what we may call the outer bark of the inspired writings, as the sap of life is present beneath the bark of the tree. If we believe that God is talking to us, we will listen.

To listen to the Word of God and to welcome it is also to open ourselves up to the life-giving force of the living Jesus. We cannot hear the Word of God without loving and adoring the Word made flesh, because they are the same. The Word of God becomes etched in our hearts in letters of fire, for it makes us burn with love. It is the Word of the Beloved, and that is why it is so important. It is the Word of the person we love, the Christ, the Word made flesh. We cannot separate the *Word* from the living person of Christ, from the burning *love* which we receive from him. The disciples on the road to Emmaus felt this:

> *Were not our hearts burning within us*
> *while he was talking to us on the road...?*
> (Lk 24:32)

Our love for the Word of God depends upon the love and adoration which we have for the one who is speaking: Jesus, the living Christ.

Respecting the Word of God

Mary respects God's Word. If the Word was made flesh in her, it was because she was ready, not only to welcome it at that moment, but to respect it all her life in the very depths of her being. Mary didn't feel, once she had given birth to Jesus, that she could forget about God's Word. She continued to respect it perfectly, as the Gospel tells us on several occasions:

> *But Mary treasured all these words*
> *and pondered them in her heart.*
> (Lk 2:19)

> *His mother treasured all these things in her heart.*
> (Lk 2:51)

Mary treasured and pondered on these things: Mary loved, for to treasure not just something, but someone – the Son of God – in her heart, means to love. We have all experienced the feeling of treasuring someone. If we look deep into our heart, the one we find is the one we love. Please God that we find the same love as Mary did: the Son of God, the Incarnate Word, who reigns in our hearts!

Mary continued to live with Jesus, within a relationship which was so strong, so deep that she knew all the joys and the sorrows of the Word made flesh. She TREASURED the Word right up until the Cross, right up to the moment when her own soul was pierced by a sword. She even continued to treasure the Word after the Cross – and this was perhaps the most difficult – so that she could pass it on to us.

We are lost in admiration and wonder before

such perfection. Treasuring the Word made flesh in such a way means living one's whole life in complete harmony with Christ.

Mary's whole life was tuned in to Christ. She followed him everywhere, not just in a symbolic sense, but literally, on a practical level. She was present during all of his hidden life: she welcomed him into her house and treasured him there, thereby becoming for us the perfect example of the most intense interior life. Then, during his public life, she accompanied Jesus on all the highways and byways. She followed him not only so that she could be by his side: this wouldn't have involved total commitment. It was so that she could make her whole life conform to that of her Son, and live his words, taking everything he did as her example so that she could imitate him in everything. It was so that she could 'configure' herself to him. For she was not content simply to hear, to listen to and receive the Word. Watching him, Mary wanted to live the Word, to put it into practice. The Word of God is Life. Mary understood this so well that she lived it throughout her whole life, and has always remained faithful.

When Jesus says: *Blessed are those who hear the word of God and obey it* (Lk 11:28), while giving us Mary his Mother as our model, he is talking to all mankind, to each one of us. He loves us and so is offering us true happiness.

Such happiness is not restricted to a particular office, or mission, or state of life. Whatever we are called to do, this happiness is offered to each of us and, we may even say, is **within the reach of each person**. What matters is not so much the task we have in life as the way we set about it. Even more important is the way in which we listen each time

God calls us in our hearts and in our lives, for each of us in our own way receives God's calls.

Jesus is really offering true happiness to each one of us: this is not just wishful thinking. We make use of our considerable imaginative skills in order to create subtle pretexts which will persuade us that these invitations from Christ are not really our concern.

The pretext used most commonly today is lack of time. But it is always possible to listen to God, even if our lives are very full. Mary, the mother of Jesus, had a great deal to do. She was poor, and the poor don't have the means to pay for help. Joseph, who has become the patron saint of workers, worked very hard. But they both listened to the Word of God and respected it. Each day they watched with love and adoration the Word made flesh.

If we listen to the Word of God we want to live it. It is not a question of changing our state of life, our occupation or our daily activities: God does not ask for this. It is a question of arranging our time and our activities so that God is always the 'first in line'. There are certain decisions which we need to make, and which require the conversion of our heart and of our thoughts. We must make these decisions, because we cannot hear the Word of God nor encounter his love and his pardon without then moving on to act, putting what we have learned into practice.

We are called to love and serve God in our everyday lives, whatever form they might take. So let's not wait for the circumstances of our lives to improve: this might never happen. We should just do our best wherever the Lord has put us. This is what ***putting it into practice*** really means.

Whatever kind of life we lead, we are all called to follow Christ. If we don't want to shy away from this calling, we will try from this moment on to follow Jesus along the road of life which he has placed before us.

Love in Adoration, a path of holiness for our time

A Christian cannot be nourished by the Eucharist without immediately wanting to put the values of the Gospel into practice. It is Jesus himself who is giving us his life and his strength in the Eucharist. He instils in us the desire to follow him and imitate him. While we are deciding how to follow him, our attention is drawn to those words he pronounced for us and which, twenty centuries later, still ring out with life and pertinence in the hearts of men and women of goodwill. There we are, at the foot of the hill, listening intently and offering up our hearts to the one who, as he speaks, is offering us these promises of happiness.

The one who is speaking is the Word, the Son of God. He is outlining a way of life for us: if we wish to follow him, we must live in poverty, showing gentleness and patience, humility and mercy, we must know how to be peacemakers and strive for justice. We must accept persecution when it comes along, and even go so far as to rejoice if we are mistreated for the sake of Christ, like the Apostles! A whole set of values which are the exact opposite of the values adopted by the world!

And yet we can feel that they are prompting surprising feelings of hope inside us, hope for a new kind of strength. The promises of the Gospel are truly 'Good News'.

Which of us hasn't experienced at least once in

our lives that feeling of emptiness and sterility in the heart which we call inner poverty? Haven't we all known moments of desperate difficulty, when we almost fall into despair? And which of us has not heard these promises of happiness echoing inside our heads:

> *Blessed are you who are poor,*
> *Blessed are you who are hungry now,*
> *Blessed are you who weep now.*
> (Lk 6:20-21)

Not one of us is guaranteed to escape severe trials in life. But at such moments, a pathway opens up before us and leads us towards the joy of the Kingdom. We all have to pass through suffering and death, in other words through the Cross: this is a concrete reality no one can escape. Christ himself took this road, in obedience to his Father.

Suffering and death are present, not so that we may be eliminated, but so that we may be resurrected with Christ! If we accept our trials wholeheartedly and offer them up, and do the same with suffering and even persecution if it arrives, all for the love of Christ, we are embodying Holiness.

This sounds rather daunting, perhaps. But we are not expected to reach the mountain top in one great leap: we can go up slowly in our own good time. Each time we take a step it is as though we are going up one more rung on a ladder: poverty, humility, purity, mercy. We shouldn't expect or want to get there straightaway. Quite the reverse: what we need is a great deal of patience. The ladder going up from earth to heaven is the path of love. The rungs of the ladder are the stages along the way, and we should go up with our feet placed carefully on each rung, our hands gripping the sides of the ladder. This is the way. And when our hearts and eyes are fixed on heaven, determined to seek the Kingdom, this is love.

So we climb gently. There is no point in trying to get up without the ladder: we won't get there. If we grasp the ladder and look downwards we'll feel dizzy and fall off. If we let go, we'll fall backwards and be smashed into smithereens. If we try to climb faster by skipping a rung, we'll lose our balance and might not be able to steady ourselves again.

There are so many pitfalls to avoid along this path of Gospel holiness. Some people – and surely this includes us? – are still at the bottom of the ladder, feeling helpless because we are frightened of hurting ourselves. When all is said and done, very few get to the top: sometimes our motivation for God and his Kingdom is lacking, or is only superficial, so is empty and fruitless, leading nowhere. Sometimes we lack perseverance or patience in our efforts, and sometimes we are only lukewarm.

So what should we do in the face of so many pitfalls? We should put our heart and soul into our efforts and keep going, knowing that our strength comes from God. It is Jesus' strength which is leading us and guiding us, as long as we look to him, for it is only with our eyes fixed on Jesus that we are able to make progress. This brings us to the crucial link with love in adoration: we have strength inside us, but it only comes from Christ.

Prayer, sacraments and our own personal efforts to put our faith into practice: all these are inextricably linked, but can only prosper, blossom and last within the context of love in adoration. For a long time, the interior life, prayer life and sacramental life have been placed in separate compartments: people have been searching for spiritual gurus, seeking new ways of praying, and looking on the sacraments as merely a devotional 'practice'. As for adoration, people hardly ever mention it and often only refer to it as a particular devotional approach. But we cannot separate these different elements, forming as they do the substance of our being and having Christ as their foundation.

Prayer linked with adoration of Jesus-Eucharist; an interior life based on the loving gaze directed towards Jesus in the Eucharist; a conversion of the heart drawn from the Heart of Christ, beating with love in the Eucharist. Love in adoration is the unchanging foundation, the cement, the link, the 'cornerstone' upon which our being is built.

Love in adoration is what unites the interior life, the prayer life, the sacramental life and the practical living of our faith. Let there be no more misrepresentation of these different aspects which interconnect and intermingle. Love in adoration of Jesus in the Eucharist, which is the source, centre and summit of our Christian life, is the pathway to holiness in our time: *a pathway of love*.

At first sight, the promises of the Gospel seem to expect a lot from us, but they are realistic and based on truth. They bring us face to face with the reality of human experience. Life forces us to discover the deepest parts of ourselves, little by little. Sooner or later it drives us into that realm of interior solitude where the all-important and ultimately personal question must be asked: do we dare to believe the one who said "Blessed are the poor, those who mourn, those who are persecuted,"? Will these words sustain us during our worst trials? Will we be able to cry, with St Paul:

> *Who will separate us from the love of Christ?*
> *Will hardship, or distress, or persecution,*
> *or famine, or nakedness, or peril, or sword?*
> *...No, in all these things we are more than*
> *conquerors*
> *through him who loved us.*
> (Rom 8:35-37)

If we remain reluctant to commit ourselves to this pathway in life, it is because we would prefer to avoid suffering. We want to run away from the cross: we want Jesus, but not his Cross! But Jesus and his Cross are *inseparable*, just as each of our lives is inseparable from suffering and death. So why should we try to avoid the inevitable? It would be better to strengthen and deepen our faith, our hope and our love by living the Gospel, by having our eyes fixed on Christ in adoration, on Christ who alone can pluck us out of suffering and death.

The cross is not the target: it is only a means, an instrument. The final aim is something else altogether: the joy of the Kingdom. Jesus himself gives us this promise in the Sermon on the Mount:

> *Blessed are the poor in spirit,*
> *for theirs is the kingdom of heaven.*
> *Blessed are the pure in heart,*
> *for they will see God.*
> *Blessed are those who are persecuted for*
> *righteousness' sake,*
> *for theirs is the kingdom of heaven.*
> (Mt 5:3-10)

How extraordinary to hear Jesus promising us his Kingdom, the Kingdom of his Father who is in heaven! We don't really appreciate, or even stop to think at all, what this means. What are difficulties, sufferings or trials in this world in comparison with the Kingdom which awaits us? St Paul draws our attention to this:

I consider that the sufferings of this present time
are not worth comparing with the glory
about to be revealed to us.
(Rom 8:18)

Jesus is offering us a Kingdom of glory with him and his Father, and longs for his Kingdom to be established in our hearts, right here on earth, straightaway. This is the request which he teaches us in the Our Father:

Thy kingdom come.
(Lk 11:2)

The reign of God alone will be the reign of glory in the world to come. But Jesus wants to set up his reign now, here on earth, in our hearts. His greatest happiness lies in establishing his sovereign reign inside us. Why are we waiting, why delay the growth of his Kingdom, why hesitate to give him all of our heart and to attract more hearts to him? Jesus seems to be saying to each of us:

"I want to reign in all hearts.
You are there, help me,
Help me to set up my Kingdom
In all hearts."[5]

Once we have understood Jesus' intense longing, we

will be drawn along the path to holiness by love alone. The path will no longer be too difficult, calling for a huge effort from us or for total perfection, for it will be a path of love.

We will not be stumbling along anymore but running with our arms outstretched. We won't be bothered by fears of being hurt or injured, nor even of our own sin which is always so heavy, slowing us down. We will join in the race, running with wild enthusiasm, spurred on not by our own feeble efforts but only by the love of Christ. Even if night sometimes falls while we are still on the road, the light of Christ will be given to us when we need it, scattered here and there to guide us day by day like a little lamp to light up each of our steps.

Oh Jesus! Help us to set up your Kingdom in our hearts from now on, and in many, many other hearts. Then you will be happy!

NOTES

1. St Ignatius of Antioch, *Epistle to the Romans,* ch. VII.
2. *The Collected Works of St. Teresa of Avila,* Vol. 3, tr. Kieran Kavanaugh O.C.D. and Otilio Rodriguez O.C.D. (ICS Publications, Washington: 1985).
3. St Augustine, *Confessions,* Book I, 1, tr. R.S. Pine-Coffin (Penguin, 1961).
4. *Confessions,* Book III, 6 and Book X, 27.
5. See *Le Mystère de l'Amour vivant,* p. 175.

3
Christ, our life

"You alone are the Holy One" [1]

Christ, the only source of holiness

We cannot find true answers to the questions we ask ourselves regarding adoration unless we know *who* it is we are adoring. So who is it we are actually adoring? This is the basic but incisive question which Jesus put to his disciples:

> *But who do you say that I am?*
> (Mk 8:29)

We are now at the heart of the problem! This is a relevant question, affecting us personally too, and we know very well that we must reply.

A veritable discovery lies ahead of us. Adoration of the Eucharist reveals to us the living person of Christ and thus leads us on the path to this discovery, which is:

- of fundamental importance because of its consequences for the life of the Church and the life of the world;
- wider in scope than the most extraordinary discoveries of the New World in the fifteenth century, or all the amazing interplanetary and cosmic discoveries of the twentieth century, and at the same time, is indicative of their full significance.

Discovering the person of Christ

Discovering Christ is vital for us and for humanity as a whole. If we have no reference points in our lives, we will lose touch with the meaning of our destiny.

Adoration of Jesus-Eucharist is the best way to bring us to this discovery. The more we adore him in silence, the more we thirst after him, and the greater is our need to find him. "Oh My Beloved, let me know you": this is the desire expressed by our soul in the depths of adoration. Jesus always grants this wish, since it was the reason for his coming. He became flesh in order to reveal himself to us and to reveal to us the Father.

Jesus is so close to us in the Eucharist, and his deepest longing is to reveal to us his person and his presence. He doesn't reveal himself to us at first as a sacrifice or as a means of nourishment, but as a *person*. This is what he did so many times with his disciples, with Mary Magdalene (*Mary!*) on Easter morning, with the disciples on the road to Emmaus when he broke the bread, and with St Paul on the road to Damascus: *I am Jesus.*

These were astounding encounters, with Jesus always appearing accompanied by light:

– the light of Easter for Mary Magdalene, on the morning of the Resurrection;
– the light which burns with a particular intensity in the hearts of the disciples on the way to Emmaus;
– the light which knocks St Paul to the ground, demonstrating the life force which radiates from Jesus' person.

This light is beyond anything which we might know. And we have a sense that we are in the presence of a mystery: the far and beyond, with all those things beyond our knowledge and understanding. The person of Christ is a mystery, but through grace and through the gift of his love, Jesus can let us enter into this mystery. He draws us in especially during adoration of the Eucharist, since this is the occasion when his presence is strongest.

Although we might enter into the mystery, this does not mean that it is possible for us to grasp the entire depths of its meaning. A mystery cannot be known, but we can come closer and closer to it, and the way of love and adoration can be the means of letting us in. So we are not talking about intellectual effort or theorising: the soul enters directly into a knowledge of God. There is a direct knowledge that God can give us of himself, a knowledge which speedily takes hold of us and which for some people, is as instant as lightning. This was the case with St Paul and, nearer to our time, with those who witnessed God's presence living and moving in a very concrete sense in their lives: Alphonse Ratisbonne, André Frossard, Didier Decoin, Paul Claudel, Charles de Foucauld and so on.[2] The list could go on and on!

Even if such an encounter is experienced in a more discreet fashion, or in any case without other people being so aware of it, it is always a decisive moment for the person concerned because it comes as an instance of amazing grace. Amos feels this when, filled with amazement, he says: "*the Lord took me from following the flock, and the Lord said to me, Go, prophesy to my people Israel*" (Am 7:15).

It is an overwhelming and amazing grace which is always God's initiative, but in which he reveals himself to the one who is seeking him. If every Christian were a true seeker and a discoverer, in other words someone intent on discovering the person of Christ, the whole Church would be transformed!

In order to make this discovery easier for us, the Lord wants to open up the pathway of Eucharistic adoration for us, and that of his own very special, distinctive Eucharistic love which I like to define as 'love in adoration'.

Love in adoration:
The special pathway to a meeting with God

Love in adoration is, in other words, love *and* adoration of the Eucharist. The essential issue is the discovery of the person of Christ in his mystery, and more precisely, in his Eucharistic mystery. For it is only the person of Christ in his entire stature, in his entire splendour, who can enable us to accomplish that great journey, the third Passover: the passage from this world to his Father and our Father.

Christ is the gateway, the way in: *I am the gate* (Jn 10:9). The gate is narrow, but it is vital to understand the correct sense of this term used by Jesus. The gate is open to all, wide open to all men and women. But there is no passage to the Father other than via the person of Christ: it is in this sense that the gate is narrow.

To be even more precise, there is no passage other than via the Eucharistic Christ, which means Christ as 'Paschal lamb'. *For our paschal lamb, Christ, has been sacrificed* (1 Cor 5:7). It is the Eucharistic Christ, it is the body and blood of Christ which are the way in, the path, the gate, the passage. This is not a Christ existing only in spirit: it is the Christ who took on our flesh, the Son of God made man who was sacrificed, who gave us his body and his blood as a gift.

The body and blood of Christ are of paramount importance for the entry into the Kingdom, for that great journey which we will undergo on the day of his return in glory.

The coming of Christ, both for the Church and for the world, is linked to the discovery in its fullest sense of the Eucharist, and to the development of the Eucharistic life of the children of God.

We are not there yet. There are so many obstacles in the way, coming from all directions. But we must work hard to get there, to bring about once and for all the reign of God, who is already among us in Christ, body and blood, living in mankind and entrusted to mankind in the Eucharist. Having given himself up to us, he is waiting for us to help him to rise up, shining in the splendour of his glory, to take us with him from this world to his Father. He will not do it without us. St Augustine tells us that he will not save us unless we participate. In the same way, he will not return without our active cooperation, our commitment. This brings us back to our responsibility and the responsibility of the whole Church to help and work towards the development of the life of Eucharistic adoration. Souls of adoration and the Houses of Adoration represent one of the ways given by God to achieve this. Sometimes they provide the means, and let us hope that they will be able to do so more and more, for God's hungry children, and for those genuine little churches which we call families, to 'let Christ come in'. This is what we are told in the *Imitation of Christ*:

"Therefore welcome Christ... When you possess Christ, you are amply rich, and He will satisfy you... Put your whole trust in God; direct your worship and love to Him alone. He will defend you...

"Here you have no abiding city, and wherever you may be, you are a stranger and a pilgrim; you will never enjoy peace until you become inwardly united to Christ... Let all your thoughts be with the Most High, and direct your humble prayers unceasingly to Christ...

"Had you but once entered perfectly into the Heart of Jesus, and tasted something of His burning love, you would care nothing for your own gain or loss."[3]

Let Christ in, so that we may live in intimacy with him. Being able, in the love of adoration, to savour a little of his ardent love! Adoration of the Eucharist allows us to experience these. Experiencing his ardent love, 'savouring' it and living it: this is the life of adoration.

By suggesting this as the life to be lived, the Houses of Adoration would like to be those ever-vigilant watchmen of the presence of Christ in the midst of mankind, offering up mankind unceasingly. They want to be on the front line of the everyday world, existing in the Church and for the Church. They are called to a vocation of silence, being set aside for God alone in adoration of the body and blood of Christ. Living this vocation in our homes allows adoration to take the world as its setting; at the same time, it allows the Church to send out feelers everywhere and to be truly present in the everyday world. *For only the real presence of Christ will be able to maintain the real presence of the Church in the everyday world.*

In this and of course in other ways, it is through the exercise of the Eucharistic life that we will participate in the coming of Jesus in glory. This return which we are awaiting is something we must desire, prepare for and work towards in a concrete manner. If we fail to do this, the Bridegroom can only be delayed: he will have no option but to wait. He cannot come without the wish and consent of his Bride, the Church. It is she who is in possession of the Eucharist: she is founded on the body of Christ and lives because of it. *The Eucharist is the living and beating heart of the Church.*

The Church must also show the Eucharist, that is, really reveal it and make its inexhaustible riches known. Just as Jesus launched himself into his public life, so should the Church provide a period of public life for Jesus-Eucharist living in the midst of mankind. Then Jesus will be able to return in a third Passover, one of glory. Jesus seems to be saying to the Church:

> I am in you, body and blood. There was no more to give, and I could not have given more love. So what are you doing with me? Are you giving me to everyone? Are you giving me to all the souls for their love and adoration? I gave myself up to mankind, giving up my life, my body and my blood. Oh my Church, my Church, why do you hesitate to show me, to give me, to place me before the loving and adoring looks of all the souls I entrusted to you? Don't be afraid. Open the gates to Jesus-Christ, to Jesus-Eucharist.

The Great Jubilee of the year 2000, an intensely Eucharistic year, should mark the launching of this preparation for a Eucharistic time, for the public life of Jesus-Eucharist. It is essential if we are to see him return in glory. Let us not miss out on this appointment, this year 2000, this entry into a new time: the 'time of the Eucharist'. The Holy Door will be opened, opening into a new stage of sacred history.

The person of Christ is unique

Nothing is comparable to the unique mystery of the person of Christ. There are two natures: the divine nature and the human nature, and yet there is only one person: Christ.

This person of Christ is unique, since there was nothing like it before and there will never be anything like it again. We are in the presence of a mystery which will never cease to amaze us. This amazement, which leaves us speechless with wonder, is in itself the beginnings of adoration. Adoring Christ means adoring him in his humanity and in his divinity at one and the same time. By taking on our flesh, Christ made God accessible to our mortal eyes. He lets us see many aspects of the mystery of God, like a crystal which sends out flashes of light from all its surfaces.

So Christ, who is such an intimate part of us, reveals God to us and only allows us to see or to catch a glimpse of as much as we can cope with. This 'feat' is brought about through the joining together of humanity and divinity, and this proximity of God is given to mankind by Christ. This is why he is truly the only mediator between God and mankind, the only way for mankind to reach God. The human nature of mankind is too fragile to see God directly: mankind needed this Man-God sent by God and being God himself, but God taking human flesh, *Light from*

Light, true God from true God, so that it could find its way to the life of the divine.

The manifestations of Christ

God's proximity to mankind was manifested to us in Christ by his Incarnation and will continue to be manifested by his Eucharistic presence, right up until his return in glory.

The first manifestation was the *Word made flesh*: Jesus, the Son of Mary, was born on Christmas morning and lived in Palestine for 30 years.

This manifestation is continued in Jesus-Eucharist: the body and blood of Jesus are entrusted to mankind in the Eucharist as evidence of his supreme love, until the end of time.

The final manifestation still to come is *Jesus in glory*, as on Mount Tabor. The apostles Peter, James and John saw him, and we too will see him as he really is. But for the time being, we are waiting for his return. Christ, who is living amongst us in the Eucharist, will manifest his person clothed in glory: the glory that he had in God's presence (St John, relating Jesus' prayer before his Passion). *So now, Father, glorify me in your own presence with the glory that I had in your presence before the world existed* (Jn 17:5). And he will make us a gift of his glory: we will share in it, be clothed in it by him. This is the undreamed of destiny to which we are all called, and once we are aware of it, we cannot remain indifferent. This is the Good News for our time, the news to proclaim, to live and to prepare for.

God has a plan, like a pathway sketched out all through the history of salvation. The person of Christ reveals himself to us little by little, more and more, to show us the way to the Father and to open up the Kingdom for us:

Jesus in Palestine Do not hold on to me… I am ascending to my Father	He want us to lift our eyes to the Father	He enters time and history in a particular geographical location
Jesus in the Eucharist We stand by our faith	He changes the nature of his presence	The Eucharist is still inside time, and inside our history. But there is no longer a single location
Jesus in glory	The Eucharist is the introduction to the Life of the Trinity	Outside time, space and history: the Life of the Kingdom.

As we progress along this path, our love and adoration should grow and develop, acquiring depth and maturity. Eucharistic love transforms us in the depths of our being in our silent union with God. We should grow in love in adoration.

Christ in his Eucharistic presence is the link

Christ's Eucharistic presence is real in the here and now for us. Adoration of Jesus-Eucharist however takes us back to Jesus of Nazareth who lived on earth 2000 years ago. At the same time, it draws the glory of the future Kingdom into us: it is linking the first and the second coming of Jesus. When we adore his body and his blood, we have an ever-increasing desire to know him better, to follow in his footsteps along the roads of Palestine. By reading the Gospel carefully we are trying to find out more about him and what he did. We would like to watch Jesus in his daily life, and to listen to him, for he is the Word, the Word of life. He is our example and we would like to model ourselves upon him, even to be like him.

If we had been living in Palestine, we would have wanted to be able to follow him on the road, watching and listening to him so that we were aware of everything he did. We would have wanted to be with him everywhere. In short, we would have wanted to live alongside him, as closely as possible, sharing his life like the Apostles, like the Virgin Mary and the holy women, who all followed him because they were totally attached to him.

But the life of Eucharistic adoration allows us to live within this attachment to the person of Christ, and to make one discovery after another. We are called to live and experience something powerful, something experienced by the first Apostles and the holy women who followed Jesus.

With Jesus-Eucharist, during adoration, we know that the person of Christ is not just an image to copy, as we might copy some celebrity. This is not enough. Christ is in himself, in his person, a treasure with infinite grace, as we well know. No one goes to him in vain. Love in adoration fills our heart and our soul with joy. All perfection is united in him, and he pours it out into us according to our ability to receive his grace. All the graces which we need for conversion and transformation come from him. This inexhaustible treasure-store of graces is like a bottomless well, and we can draw from it to our heart's content. It is the spring of living water which never runs dry, promised to the Samaritan woman. When we confront all this richness, this endless and infinite richness, we know that we have met the Messiah, the Son of God, in whom all holiness exists.

Because he is God, and Son of God, the source of holiness is in him. When we come to bathe in his love during adoration, we are bathing in the very holiness of God. So why should we seek holiness elsewhere than in the person of Christ? It is Jesus who came to reveal the Father to us, through the gift of the Holy Spirit, the Spirit of holiness. He reveals to us the very holiness of God. Adoration of the living person of Jesus in the Eucharist has clearly become the most direct and certain path of holiness open to us.

Since love in adoration is Christ-centred, it brings together different elements which are often separated, and thus avoids the development of an interior life simply for its own sake, existing in a world of its own and taking up much time and effort. The interior life we speak of can never be separated from the loving, burning and life-giving gaze of adoration which falls each day on the living person of Christ. This same gaze of adoration leads us to develop a sacramental life. It guides our life: it is the passage our life is following.

A marvellous sense of unity is found through love in adoration. It is a path which unites all of our being and is:

– sure, because attached to Christ: it is the best antidote to sects;

- direct, since there is no intermediary;
- a shortcut – which is what most people want nowadays.

We have no time to lose, and must stop taking those other long, roundabout routes. We cannot spend our whole life going round in circles rather than going straight to our destination. The Gospel needs to be spread and we must hurry: the Good News must be proclaimed without delay. If we refuse to hurry up, there will be thousands more years of waiting. The Good News means:

- proclaiming Christ,
- saying his name,
- revealing his person and his presence.

It is as simple as that, and yet we have made things so complicated!

> Lord, teach us to be simple.
> Let us discover your simplicity, your oneness.
> Teach us not to waste any more time.
> Put us on the direct path
> Which leads us to you.
> This path is YOU.

We are waiting for that final moment, that major event, that meeting point between the history of God and mankind: "we proclaim your death, Lord Jesus, until you come in glory" (Eucharistic prayer). We are longing for that moment, and we must always be aware of preparing for it, hastening its progress. It depends upon us and upon the entire Church. It is our personal responsibility and the responsibility of the entire Church.

We are of course waiting for this event. But during this waiting period, we are aware that it is the Eucharist which ensures the continuity of the living presence of Christ on earth. There is a continuity between the first coming of Jesus on earth, the Incarnate Word, and his second coming on the day of his return in his glorified human nature. And this continuity is ensured by the Eucharist, the living presence of Jesus among mankind. There is a continuity in the life of Christ: he is still living among us. His manner of being present differs, but his presence is continuous and permanent.

It is not and cannot be a passive presence. The presence of Jesus living among us is the presence of God: Father, Son and Holy Spirit. It is an active presence, bubbling with life and Resurrection. It is a dynamic presence which leads us with a power which is at present held in check, but which is sure and unlike any other power. It is leading us to the culminating and inescapable event in the history of mankind: the return in glory of the person of Christ.

The consuming fire of the Spirit is unceasingly at work, like the ball of fire at the centre of the earth. This consuming fire is blazing away and spreading out invisibly for the time being but, like the flames of an erupting volcano, it will leap up into the air when all is ready, at the time decided by the Father. It will reveal to us the Father.

The Son Incarnate will show himself to us, in all his glory. Only he, the sole mediator as always, will be able to bring us into the glory of the Father, so that we may have Life, and Life in abundance.

Taking a panoramic view like this, we can see the extraordinary importance of the Eucharist as the living presence of Christ among mankind. This continuity, this permanent living presence among mankind is a sign of God's ineffable love for us! This aspect of the Eucharist as the living presence of Christ among mankind cannot be ignored: its significance should be understood so that we may prepare for the return of Christ.

There would be neither sacrifice nor nourishment if there had not first been the Word made flesh, the person of Jesus, taking on our flesh, and then his living presence, body and blood, in the Eucharist. His person precedes the sacrifice and the Bread of life: the Incarnation necessarily precedes the Redemption. And the consecrated bread and wine are only the body and blood of Christ because he gave up his life. His person and his presence exist for all eternity, but the sacrifice and nourishment will pass away. There will be no more sacrifice in the Kingdom because suffering and death will exist no more, and nourishment will not exist because our glorified bodies will not have the same needs as fleshly bodies. But the person of Christ, the presence of God inhabiting all of the holy city, all of the Kingdom, will still remain eternally PRESENT.

The reign of God will be the spreading out of his presence. It will fan out everywhere and spread forever, and there will be nothing to stop it. When this happens, we will be alive, we will be there.

Christ will always be the person who IS:

Before Abraham was, I AM.
(Jn 8:58)

He is always the one who is because he is God. When we see him face to face, we will rejoice in his presence eternally. Loving and adoring him in the Eucharist is our way of rejoicing *through him, with him, in him,* rejoicing in this presence which he gives us already on earth, unceasingly, freely, through pure love. He who is all love delights in being here among the children of mankind.

This rejoicing is only a reflection of his love. We can show him our joy, send it to back him again in the love of adoration: the joy of grace and thanksgiving. In this meeting of adoration, the soul gives thanks to God because he is God, because he is there, because he is PRESENT in our presence.

In the action of loving and adoring, the soul is experiencing the joy of meeting God, of having an intimate exchange with him. By giving thanks to God during adoration, the soul is "in the Eucharist", and is celebrating the Eucharist. This is how adoration prepares for and prolongs the sacrifice of the Mass, extending and perpetuating it.

The Holy Sacrifice takes only a certain amount of time. But the time given to thanksgiving, carried out in love and adoration, has no limits. Thanksgiving may be carried out all the time, everywhere, as the apostle Paul says:

> *...present your bodies as a living sacrifice,*
> *holy and acceptable to God,*
> *which is your spiritual worship.*
> (Rom 12:1)

This aspect of the Eucharist will never stop. It is not limited by history either, since it will continue in the life of the Kingdom. The liturgy in heaven will be endless adoration.

Adoration of the Eucharist reminds us unceasingly, brings back our 'memory' – *Do this in memory of me* – that Jesus is fully man and fully God. We can adore him in the species of consecrated bread and wine because he became man. We can adore him in this mystery of the Eucharist because he is God. The Eucharistic mystery is the mystery of the Man-God, and when we adore Jesus-Eucharist we remind ourselves unceasingly of this fact. Our faith is thus rooted in and directed towards the truth. In these times when so many errors, false beliefs and sects surround us, the life of adoration of the Eucharist is the sure pathway for our faith, our hope and our love. It is the way of holiness for our times and I would go so far as to say, the *only* way of holiness because it is fixed on the person of Christ, the only source of holiness:

> *For you alone are the Holy One,*
> *You alone are the Lord,*
> *You alone are the Most High,*
> *Jesus Christ.*[4]

The Body and Blood of Christ, the only pathway

The body of Christ, like every human body, is made up of flesh and blood: two distinct and singular, real items. We have here a very concrete description of the person of Christ. Jesus himself provides this very realistic descriptive detail in the Gospel when he proclaims himself and offers himself as the Bread of Life:

> *Those who eat my flesh and drink my blood*
> *have eternal life,*
> *and I will raise them up on the last day;*
> *for my flesh is true food*
> *and my blood is true drink.*

*Those who eat my flesh and drink my blood
abide in me, and I in them...
This is the bread which came down from heaven,
not like that which your ancestors ate,
and they died.
But the one who eats this bread will live forever.*
(Jn 6:54-58)

We can imagine the shocking effect of these words of Jesus on those who were listening. On a logical level, they made no sense. The meaning was on another level: within the mystery of love, accessible only by faith. Some of those listening were scandalised: *How can this man give us his flesh to eat?* (Jn 6:52).

Despite all the references and comparisons with bread, despite Jesus' words identifying himself as the Bread of Life, it is not until the Last Supper on Holy Thursday that the final explanation is given, when Jesus takes the bread, breaks it and gives it to his disciples saying:

Take, eat; this is my body.
(Mt 26:26)

Jesus gives his body – which will be given up to the cross the following day – as nourishment and in the form of bread. Jesus gives his blood, shed for all men, in the form of wine. It still needed thinking about! It is God's decision: so simple, and presented so simply. Simplicity is the hallmark of God.

*Drink from it, all of you;
for this is my blood...*
(Mt 26:26)

So his blood and his body were made available to

all, thanks to that 'convenient' initiative of using bread and wine, the daily food and drink of ordinary people.

There is nothing extravagant or scandalous in this, then, but only the proof given to mankind of God's love for them. Love is ingenious, and thus gave birth to the Eucharist. It is an everlasting and inexhaustible gift, for we can draw all we like from this infinite Eucharistic mystery:

- The Eucharist can never perish while there is still bread and wine on earth, and while the priestly ministry still gives us the body and blood of Christ, as if newly-born.
- The Eucharist can never run out because it is the mystery of the love of Christ. We can draw from it with all our strength for the whole of our life, like the Samaritan woman at the well:

> *If you knew the gift of God,*
> *and who it is that is saying to you,*
> *'Give me a drink',*
> *you would have asked him,*
> *and he would have given you living water.*
> (Jn 4:10)

The Eucharist is now revealed and proclaimed, and it is Jesus who gives himself both as a spring which will never run dry, and as the only harbour for true adoration. There is no point in asking ourselves whether our adoration should take place on Mount Garizim, where the Samaritans worshipped, or in the Temple at Jerusalem like the Jews. The adoration of the living God is not restricted to any one particular place.

Only Jesus can lead us, through his person, to true adoration "in spirit and in truth". No one can adore the Father if they do not adore the Son, if they have not experienced that personal meeting with the person of Christ, Son of Man and Son of God. Adoration of the Father is by way of the person of the Son, through the discovery of the person of Christ who gives himself to us as Bread of Life and as source of life. This is how he comes to be PRESENT in a very real manner in the Eucharist, man and God. What is more, when we receive communion the priest utters these striking words:

> The body of Christ.

and when we take communion under both kinds:

> The body and the blood of Christ.

In giving us Christ, he identifies him, presents him and then entrusts him to us. At the same instant, it seems to me that a 'loving attraction' occurs: like the little needle irresistibly attracted to the magnet in a compass. For if the priest identifies the Eucharist as being the body of Christ, he is also identifying us. It is as though he is introducing us to each other. For

> "we are the body of Christ;
> we are the blood of Christ."

In receiving his body and his blood, we become that which we receive. The Church also bears this beautiful name of the Body of Christ, for this is what she is, and this is the Church's prime responsibility. The Church must account for the body and the blood of Jesus, and will have to do so at the end of time:

> "What have you done to me?"

Thus the body and the blood of Christ are at the heart of the individual lives of each of us, at the heart of the history of the Church and of the history of salvation.

But what does the body of Christ really mean for us? Or the blood of Christ? In other words, the question facing us is:

> "And you, yourself,
> who do you say I am?"

Here are a few thoughts.

The word Passover (and the adjective Paschal) means passage. A passage necessarily involves a starting point and an ending, or a departure and an arrival, or an entry and an exit. There is a connection between the two, a continuity, and it is this continuity which forms the passage:

- at the start, there are preparations
- at the end, there is a transformation
- between the two, there is a path. This path, either in a geographical sense or in time, is transitory but essential. It is this which provides the connection or the continuity between the entry and the exit, between the departure and the arrival.

There are thus three aspects to this passage:

- a preparation
- a transformation
- a continuous link allowing the movement from the first point to the second.

The passage thus allows access to a new point and to arrive at a surprising transformation. *Christ, our*

Paschal (Passover) Lamb is the unique and perfect example. He allows us unceasing access from this world to his Father, accomplishing this extraordinary passage:

- from darkness into the splendour of his light;
- from death to Life;
- from slavery to freedom;
- from sin to holiness;
- from this earthly time to the Kingdom.

> *I am making all things new,*
> *says the Lord:*
> *A new heaven and a new earth.*
> (Rev 21:1,5)

Within the unique Passover which is the body of Christ, we can make out three stages, which I would like to call the three Passovers for the sake of clarity:

- the traditional Passover of the Jews;
- the new and eternal Passover of Holy Thursday;
- the final Passover, which is still to come and is eschatological, in other words, to do with the last things. This is the Passover of the return in glory, which will bring us into the Kingdom.

The Traditional Passover

The traditional Jewish Passover represented a long period of preparation before the radical transformation effected by the coming of Christ. The Passover was a reminder, a memorial to the passage across the Red Sea. This passage across the Red Sea allowed the Hebrew people:

- to leave the land of exile and journey towards the Promised Land;
- to leave a life of slavery and head for freedom;
- to escape death, and to know salvation;

all through the blood of the lamb wiped onto the door lintels. On that famous night which preceded the departure from the land of exile, the blood of the lamb prefigured the blood of Christ which would be shed for the salvation of not only the Jews, but of all: *For our Paschal Lamb, Christ, has been sacrificed* (1 Cor 5:7).

This is a prophecy of the gift of the Eucharist, the body and blood of Christ, the true Lamb who marks the passage from the Old to the New Testament. It took thousands of years of preparation in the desert, and in the history of the Jewish people, before the radical transformation could be effected with the coming of Christ.

Throughout all this time, the sense of continuity was protected because the Messiah was awaited. The Living God continued to prepare the Jewish people for the coming of Christ, through the voices of the prophets and through his own direct and frequent intervention.

The New Passover

It was the coming of Christ on Christmas morning which brought about the new Passover, the new passage, promised by the prophets for more than 4,000 years. What an immensely long time for mankind to wait: perhaps a long time for God, too!

It is a passage from the Old to the New Testament, and a passage from the old world to the new world.

Everything has changed now. This radical change brings with it the need for a transformation in our mentality, a new way of looking at things: in short, a conversion of the heart.

The new Passover is here in the Eucharist, made real and given to us. The consecrated bread is the body of Christ, the consecrated wine is the blood of Christ. The Bread of Life lets us pass from earthly life to the eternal life, from the Old Covenant to the New, in order to bring us into the life of glory. And this brings us back to our three Passovers.

All this painstaking preparation within the never-ending continuity of waiting for Christ, thus finds its realisation in the gift which Christ gives us in the Eucharist, the gift of his body and his blood. There is a realisation, but there is also simultaneously a new departure: a new life lived in the unceasing and increasingly ardent expectation of Christ in glory.

Starting with this presence of Christ hidden in the Eucharist, we are now once more waiting for that great event proclaimed and promised by Jesus himself: his return in glory.

The Third Passover

When Christ who is your life is revealed,
then you also will be revealed with him in glory.
(Col 3:4)

This new time of waiting assumes a particular importance for us and for the entire Church, for the Eucharist, the body and blood of Christ, is like the passage stretching out ahead of us, which we must take in order to go:

- from this earthly and mortal life to eternal life;
- from our baptism to our entry into glory;
- and it is the Eucharist again which ensures the continuity of the real presence of Jesus, from the time of his earthly life up to his coming in glory.

There will be a personal passage for each of us: our death. Jesus calls us through our death, and comes himself to find us. It will be a magnificent encounter if we allow ourselves to be drawn into his light, but still an encounter hidden to everyone else, to the world in general, since our bodies will play no part in this particular passage. There will still be a time of waiting. There will be more to come, and this will happen at the final Passover promised to us with the return of Jesus in glory. We are preparing for a new passage of Jesus amongst us, a new Passover which will complete and fulfil the Passover of Holy Thursday, the Passover of every Eucharistic celebration.

While we are waiting for this amazing event, the return of Jesus, who will lead us little by little towards a radical change in our attitudes, we suffer here on earth, for we are longing for this new world in which there will be no more tears or sorrow.

But all those countless souls who have gone before us are also longing for that moment when their souls will finally be reunited with their bodies: their resurrected, immortal and glorified bodies. For the human being was created body and soul by God, and cannot know true happiness as long as the body and the soul remain separated through death. So there is an immense and mysterious sense of yearning and expectation on the part of all those who are dead, joining forces with ours here on earth. The living and the dead are united in their longing for the coming of Christ in glory, for only then will we know our true destiny: we will enter body and soul into the glory promised us, the glory which is Christ's glory.

There will also be the passage of the entire Church from this world into the other, from this temporal world into the eternal Kingdom, on the day of Jesus' return in glory. This encounter between the Church and the person of Christ in glory will take place in full view of everyone.

At that moment we will understand the full meaning of Christ coming like a Bridegroom at last to join his Bride, his Church, for a perfect, indissoluble and endless union. He will join his Bride who throughout her earthly life has been living for and through the presence of the Bridegroom, his body and blood in the Eucharist.

The Church herself uses the beautiful expression, '*real presence*', to describe the Most Blessed Sacrament. There is no better way of putting it. This real presence of Jesus in our midst is so consoling. On the day of his Ascension, Jesus did not leave us alone, and said so to the disciples:

> *I will not leave you orphaned;*
> *I am coming to you.*
> (Jn 14:18)

It is true that Jesus sent his Spirit in a special way on the day of Pentecost. But the power of the Spirit is also particularly active during the celebration of each Eucharist. When the priest celebrates Mass, he invokes the Holy Spirit before each consecration and asks him to come. The love of the Father, of the Son and of the Holy Spirit is thus altogether directed towards mankind, realising once again the presence of Jesus, body and blood, on the altar, so that he may be given to mankind as food for eternal life.

Thus, the Eucharist ensures a continuous and permanent presence of Jesus in the midst of mankind.

This presence may even be said to be our proof that he will return in glory, for when Jesus returns it will be in his own person, but clothed in his glorified body. We will see him as he is (cf. *St John*). It will be the person of Christ, Jesus, again and for always: Jesus the Son of God and the Son of Man, who will be visible to our eyes. During his earthly life, Jesus looked like any other man. *He had to become like his brothers and sisters in every respect,* St Paul tells us (Heb 2:17). Jesus took on our human condition so completely that his divine nature was imperceptible, except through the eyes of faith, or to the eyes of those who perceived it when he was on Mount Tabor. Many, many people were unaware of his divinity. They said: *He is the son of Mary and of Joseph, the carpenter,* meaning that such a man could not be the Son of God.

It is because people did not recognise him as God that they put him on the cross: *This man blasphemes.* But Jesus asked them to see what he had done: miracles and all kinds of healings which testified to the divine power in him. Those who crucified him, however, wanted to see concrete results. No doubt they were expecting prodigious feats of human achievement in the temporal world: illustrious deeds which would have dazzled everyone. But Jesus told them: *My kingdom is not from this world* (Jn 18:36).

What a revolutionary change in attitude was needed in those days, and what a revolutionary change in attitude is still needed today: one which will keep prompting us to move from the temporal level to the spiritual level! We might not be angels, but we could still become aware that the temporal world is only a springboard to launch us into the spiritual world.

Jesus serves as an example of this for us. He is not purely spirit, since as the Son of God, he became a man. Jesus will never be purely spirit. He will remain clothed in his glorified body throughout all eternity, everlastingly retaining both his human and his divine natures. All the mystery of the person of Christ is contained in this wonder of wonders.

We are talking about a prodigy: an exceptional human being. Many people refused to accept him as such, since there was no glamour or visible splendour. The most dazzling brilliant light was revealed, however, to Peter, James and John on Mount Tabor, the three who entered into the presence of glory when the cloud enveloped them.

And yes, this prodigious human being is there still, until the end of time, in the Eucharist. For Jesus-Man is present in it. This presence would not be possible however if this Jesus-Man were not at the same time Jesus-God, containing within himself all the force of life and Resurrection which belongs only to God.

Countless numbers of people today fail to accept this, sadly, for there is no visible splendour accompanying Jesus in the Eucharist, either. But what if all Christians, every one of the baptised, came together to live within the amazing wonder of this mystery! Living in adoration of the mystery of the person of Christ in the Eucharist! Living in adoration of the mystery of his Love living in us and among us until the end of time, in his Eucharist!

Such ardent and unceasing adoration is far from evident today. And yet we could live in adoration if we wished, through the grace of God, participating in its development and helping to spread it further and further.

Such a way of living would be an anticipation of the coming of Jesus in glory, and we would be preparing for it. The time of preparation for the return of Christ in glory should be a ***Eucharistic time***. In this sense, adoration of the body and blood of Jesus in the Eucharist includes an anticipation of his return, a kind of preparation and making ready carried out with the deepest longing.

Love in adoration is a herald of the face-to-face encounter awaiting us in the life of glory, and this life of glory can only be reached through the body and blood of Jesus. Now we can understand Jesus' description of himself:

I am the way, and the truth, and the life.
(Jn 14:6)

Yes, the living person of Jesus in the Eucharist is the sovereign way leading us from death to life, and to a life which never ends. It is the same sovereign way which leads us from this earthly world into the Kingdom which is not of this world. Just as, when Jesus passed from this world to his Father he became the Eucharist, we too must do as he did, and do it with him: take the sovereign way of the Eucharist in order to pass from this world to our heavenly Father. ***We must become a Eucharistic Church***.

The Church, which has the Eucharist within her, is proceeding towards a new intervention from God: the return of the person of Jesus in his glory. All we have to do is trust in him, and we know we will find the way. We will find the way within the context of a life given to the Eucharist, and through such a life we will *pass with Christ from this world to his Father.*

NOTES

1. From the *Gloria*.
2. Frossard and Claudel were twentieth-century French Catholic writers: Decoin is a contemporary French Catholic writer.
   Ratisbonne was a Jew who visited Rome in 1842 and converted to Catholicism following a vision of the Blessed Virgin. He became a Jesuit and settled in the Holy Land, devoting his life to the conversion of Jews and Muslims.
   Charles, Viscount of Foucauld, was a French army officer who became a Trappist following his conversion in 1886. He later lived as a solitary hermit, serving the poor in Algeria, and was murdered in an anti-French uprising in 1916.
3. Thomas à Kempis, *The Imitation of Christ,* tr. Leo Sherley-Price (Penguin Classics, 1952).
4. From the *Gloria*.

4
Eternal Adoration

"The glory of God is man and woman fully alive, and the life of mankind is the vision of God."[1]

The Lamb

The person of Christ is on many occasions in the Scriptures compared with a Lamb, and described as *the Lamb of God*.

The Lamb, however, is always linked to sacrifice. He gives his life and, more precisely, he sheds his blood: how precious is the blood of the Lamb! It is the cause of our salvation.

The figure of the Lamb helps us to appreciate the Eucharistic mystery. Because he is linked to sacrifice, the lamb is always at the same time linked to our adoration. The figure of the Lamb thus enables us to enter more deeply into the life of adoration.

And finally, the figure of the Lamb brings us back to the three Passovers. These are:

- the lamb of the Old Testament
- the Christ, 'Lamb of God', presented by John the Baptist
- the Lamb of Revelation, a portrayal which casts much light on what the life of the Kingdom will be like.

This progression still revolves around the person of Christ. As with the three Passovers, we can see the major step forward that God urges upon humanity, through these three figures of the Lamb. God chooses a path of patience and fidelity, taking by the hand our sinful humanity which is heading for death, in order to lead us through Christ right up to the transfiguration into the eternal Kingdom.

The Lamb of the Old Testament

For the Hebrew people, celebrating the Passover meant sacrificing a lamb. Here we find a prefiguration of the true Easter Passover.

The lamb which appeared in front of Abraham in order to spare his son Isaac was equally a herald of the true Easter Passover. God did not want Abraham to sacrifice his son. But it was a prefiguration, a declaration coming from the Father who would give up his Son. It was the most precious gift possible, and the most heart-wrenching. The gift was unconditional and all-encompassing, and so it was the gift of a life: flesh and blood.

Abraham's lamb, caught in the thorns of the thicket – as Jesus taking up our sins would be covered in thorns during his Passion – is given by God. This sacrifice is greater than any other, and its implications are vast.

In presenting Abraham with a lamb, the living God was indicating that he would give his own Son like a lamb, that is, as a sacrifice: a sacrifice so entire that it would involve both body and blood. For we can die without actually shedding our blood.

But with Christ there is an absolute gift, with both his body being given up and his blood being shed. There is no more to give.

> *Having loved his own who were in the world,*
> *He loved them to the end.*
> (Jn 13:1)

Before the coming of Christ, the prophets had also on many occasions prophesied the sacrifice of Christ. Isaiah provides the best image of the lamb destined for sacrifice, in his striking description of the suffering servant:

> *See, my servant shall prosper;*
> *he shall be exalted and lifted up,*
> *and shall be very high.*
> *Just as there were many who were astonished at him*
> *– so marred was his appearance,*
> *beyond human semblance,*
> *and his form beyond that of mortals –*
> *so shall he startle many nations...*
> *For he grew up before him like a young plant,*
> *and like a root out of dry ground;*
> *he had no form or majesty that we should look at him,*
> *nothing in his appearance that we should desire him.*
> *He was despised and rejected by others;*
> *a man of suffering and acquainted with infirmity;*
> *and as one from whom others hide their faces*
> *he was despised and we held him of no account.*
> *But he was wounded for our transgressions,*
> *crushed for our iniquities;*
> *upon him was the punishment that made us whole,*
> *and by his bruises we are healed...*
> *He was oppressed, and he was afflicted,*
> *yet he did not open his mouth;*
> *like a lamb that is led to the slaughter,*
> *and like a sheep that before its shearers is silent,*
> *so he did not open his mouth.*
> (Isa 52:13-15 and 53:2-7)

The face of Christ during his Passion is already sketched out for us in this prophecy. This Lamb is so meek and gentle! He lets his accusers do what they will, and says nothing. He doesn't resist or complain. He suffers it all: insults and humiliation, pain and maltreatment, all without a word, in silence and humility.

We cannot help thinking of how Jesus was to describe himself later: *I am gentle and humble in heart* (Mt 11:29). These are without any doubt the two highest and most admirable virtues, since they come from the Heart of Christ! Jesus speaks to us about them because he wants us to love them and imitate them. Gentleness and humility are so desirable: they are the two qualities we must acquire in love and in adoration of the Eucharist: they unite us with the Heart of Christ. **Gentleness and humility, the fruits of love in adoration**: if we could little by little live these qualities more fully, how the world could be changed!

Christ, Lamb of God

The person who really proclaimed the Messiah, as Lamb of God, was John the Baptist, "the greatest among the children of men" according to Jesus' own words.

> *Here is the Lamb of God*
> *who takes away the sins of the world!*
> (Jn 1:29)

This is how John the Baptist describes Jesus to his own disciples. Something entirely new is happening, and the image of the lamb takes on an unexpected significance. It reveals to us certain aspects of the mystery of the person of Christ, throwing them into a new light: a light which could only be seen with the arrival of Christ.

When John the Baptist sees Christ and cries: *Here is the Lamb of God*, he too is proclaiming that Christ has come to give his life in sacrifice. But this lamb is no ordinary lamb: it is the Lamb of God, in other words the Lamb sent by God the Father who gives up his Son.

He is the one who takes away the sins of the world. His sacrifice is not short-lived nor without consequence. This Lamb who takes away the sins of the world can only be God, sent from God, for only God may free mankind from sin.

In some way the mystery of the Son of God made man is revealed to John the Baptist, and he proclaims it to us. By doing this, he proclaims the unheard-of good news of our freedom: the freedom of the world from the sin which is weighing it down.

Christ, the Lamb of God, comes to take away, to wipe out, to remove not just individual **sins** but **the sin** of the world. He is the true liberator who will take away this immense weight which bears down on humanity. Only Christ, the Lamb of God, could undertake such a task. So the Old Testament notion of sacrifice is now largely forgotten. The Messiah is the Saviour, and comes to liberate the world.

God, the living God, the God of our fathers, liberator of Israel, becomes through his Son a God the Father who is a liberator of all humanity: all humanity whom he loves just as a father loves his child.

But there is even more: this sacrifice accomplished by Christ, the Lamb of the Father, is a unique sacrifice because he is perfection itself. There has never been a sacrifice like this before, and there never will be again. From that moment on, all the offerings and animal sacrifices become null and void. The body of Christ is the true Lamb, and the blood of Christ shed for us is the source of our salvation.

The love of God does not stop even there. Because this sacrifice is unique, it is accomplished once for all time. So it must be prolonged in time, it must always be current at every moment, and it must be fully effective at each instant. It is through an absolute miracle of the love of God that this perfect and unique sacrifice is unceasingly renewed, and is offered again and again right up to the end of time in the Holy Sacrifice of the Mass, through the mystery of the Eucharist.

Each Eucharistic celebration makes present, unfolding before us, that priceless gift given to mankind of the body and blood of Jesus, who became for us the true Lamb, the Passover Lamb.

It is the Passover Lamb who gives his body to be eaten in the form of bread; the Passover Lamb who gives his blood as a drink in the form of wine. His body is given up and his blood is shed unceasingly in the Eucharist, until the end of the world, until Jesus comes in glory.

When this happens, it will be the absolute and eternal Eucharist: the true Passover will have arrived at its fulfilment. The Lamb of God, who takes away the sins of the world, will have completed his mission. He is the one who will take us into the Kingdom of glory. It is *through him, with him and in him* that we will gain entry. So we will live in an eternal Eucharist, or in other words, in a state of eternal thanksgiving which will be an endless state of adoration.

The Lamb of God is linked to the Eucharist and to our adoration

Before he gives communion to the faithful, each priest says these words:

*This is the Lamb of God
who takes away the sins of the world.*

These words of John the Baptist are therefore part of the liturgy of the Mass, and are spoken by the priest as he shows the faithful the body of Christ in the form of consecrated bread.

The Lamb of God is given as food for eternal life because he gave himself as a sacrifice and was offered as a victim, shedding his blood in order to obtain salvation for us.

There is a connection here between baptism and the Eucharist: we are struck by the fact that it is the words of John, the one who baptised in the Jordan, which are taken up during each Eucharistic communion.

When we are about to take communion, we can direct all our attention to Jesus whom we receive in the Eucharist by loving and adoring him as the Lamb of God. This will give our love in adoration, in this mystery of the Lamb, a special tenderness for Jesus who is submissive and obedient in all respects to his Father's will, and gentle and humble towards mankind, to whom he offers the greatest gift possible: that of his life. If we do this, we will avoid saddening him by attaching so little importance to him, as the prophet Isaiah says: *He was despised and we held him of no account* (Isa 53:3). We so often take no account of him! That is why the prayers, vigils and burning, consuming love of souls in adoration are so precious to the Heart of God.

Through his sacrifice, the Lamb of God sheds his blood. He purifies us of our sins and takes away the sin of the world. Henceforth we are baptised in the blood of Christ, the blood of the Lamb. This is what John the Baptist was proclaiming.

It is also in the blood of Christ that our sins are forgiven in the sacrament of reconciliation. We ask forgiveness from the Lamb of God, and it is through him that we obtain forgiveness: *Lamb of God, you take away the sins of the world: have mercy on us.* And it is in the blood of Christ that we are *eucharised*, for we drink our fill from the source of eternal life.

The Lamb of God thus gives himself in sacrifice for the forgiveness of sins, but what is even more, he gives himself in order to give us the source of life, eternal life. All the mysteries of the person of Christ and of his mission among mankind are contained in this expression, Lamb of God. This is why the Lamb is so worthy of our adoration.

Christ's presence in the book of Revelation as the Lamb tells us that, when we are in the Kingdom, we will remember that Christ is the one who has saved us.

We will not be able to forget for a moment that Christ, the Lamb of God, has shed his blood for us and that our share in the Kingdom is through this precious blood. Without the blood of Christ, the blood of the Lamb, we would not be experiencing the joy that will come to those who are saved. We will not be able to stop ourselves adoring the one who saves, not for a single moment… What immense joy there is in this certain knowledge! We sometimes find it very difficult now to keep ourselves in a state of adoration, but we will do it perfectly through the pure grace obtained from the blood of the Lamb.

The more importance we attach to the body and blood of Christ during our adoration in our earthly life, the more fully will we participate in that immense proclamation of adoration, bathed in indescribable peace and joy, which will issue from all those who are saved. It will be an adoration so full of love that we will enter into the mystery of the love of the Trinity, into a life of perfect union with our God, the living God.

This is what we sing during Mass in the *Gloria*:

Lord Jesus Christ, only Son of the Father,
Lord God, Lamb of God,
you take away the sin of the world:
have mercy on us;
you are seated at the right hand of the Father:
receive our prayer.
For you alone are the Holy One,
you alone are the Lord.

This acclamation is the most beautiful expression of sung adoration. What else can we say to the Lamb of God, the Son of God made man, than this prayer:

For you alone are the Holy One,
you alone are the Lord,
you alone are the Most High,
Jesus Christ.

The Lamb of Revelation

The theme of the Lamb is frequently taken up in the book of Revelation, and always linked to adoration.

This makes it clear to us what life in the Kingdom of God will be like. We will bow down with the angels and the elders before the throne of the Lamb and sing unceasingly to his glory in the heavenly liturgy:

> *After this I looked,*
> *and there was a great multitude*
> *that no one could count,*
> *from every nation, from all tribes and peoples*
> *and languages,*
> *standing before the throne*
> *and before the Lamb,*
> *robed in white,*
> *with palm branches in their hands.*
> *They cried out in a loud voice, saying,*
> *Salvation belongs to our God*
> *who is seated on the*
> *throne, and to the Lamb!*
> (Rev 7:9-10)

We will recognise him as such: the Son of God made man, sacrificed for us like a lamb, but resurrected and glorified. We will adore him in a communion of eternal love for we will never cease to be aware that he has brought us salvation.

It is in the Eucharist that the person of Christ is most obviously the Lamb of God. So, in order to prepare ourselves for the life of adoration which we will have in the Kingdom, it is right and necessary in this earthly life to love and adore the Lamb of God, who takes away the sin of the world, in the Eucharistic person of Christ. But we are also loving and adoring the Lamb of God who reigns on the throne, and before whom the great multitude stand, serving him day and night.

There can be no doubt that this unceasing 'service' given to the Son of man is adoration. To serve the Lamb of God day and night is to serve him by loving him and adoring him with that love which is so precious to him: ***love in adoration***.

Once again, the words of the liturgy of the Mass join forces with the heavenly liturgy in the same, single impulse of adoration:

> *Father, all-powerful and ever-living God,*
> *we do well always and everywhere to give*
> *you thanks*
> *through Jesus Christ our Lord.*

The Body of Christ and its eternal wounds

When Jesus appears to his apostles after his Resurrection, they are so stupefied that he is obliged to prove to them that he is neither a ghost nor a hallucination. He eats bread and fish with them by the lakeside, and is also recognised by them during a meal, as he breaks the bread, in the well-known episode with the disciples going to Emmaus. On another occasion he shows them his wounds. St Thomas, who is wondering whether he is seeing things, is invited by Jesus to *Put your finger here...* Jesus wants him to be reassured by his sense of touch that his eyes are not deceiving him. Then St Thomas believes, and his act of faith prompts this cry of adoration: *My Lord and my God!* (Jn 20:28).

Each time we recognise in faith that Jesus is God, we are carrying out an act of adoration. Our faith fills us with wonder and makes us want to bow down before such love: in a word, to adore.

St Thomas adores the person of the risen Christ, and recognises him as Man and God. He is a man because he has a body which can be touched, but he is not just any man. This is the Jesus whom the apostles have followed during his earthly life, the Jesus who suffered and was nailed to the cross. The body of this man bears the mark of the wounds of the one who was crucified. His hands and feet are pierced, and so, as irrefutable proof, is his Heart.

The Heart of Christ was pierced by a spear. If ever it had been possible to confuse Jesus with another victim of crucifixion, the wound in the Heart proves that the Resurrected One is truly Jesus of Nazareth: *the one whom they have pierced.*

Thomas and no doubt the surrounding apostles adore the body of the risen Christ at this extraordinarily moving point, but at the same time, they also feel immense love and adoration for the five wounds. The glorified body of Jesus bears – as the mark of glory (true glory) – the five wounds through which he gave us all, and gave us so much: his life.

> *No one has greater love than this,*
> *to lay down one's life for one's friends.*
> (Jn 15:13)

So with St Thomas and all the apostles we find ourselves, in an act of faith, adoring the body of the risen Jesus, marked for all time by the five wounds. We remain dumbstruck in amazement: the glorified body of Christ, after his Resurrection, bears the mark of the five wounds. When we adore the body of Christ, we are therefore adoring his wounds, and we will do so for all eternity! In short, we will always see the wounds marking the body of Christ when we adore him. They will forever remind us that he offered himself, that he was put on the Cross, that his side was pierced in order to bring us salvation: and that he shed his blood through each of his wounds, including his Heart.

We are saved by him, because he took on our flesh, he clothed himself in our humanity. He took the body of a man, and lowered himself even to death, and death on a cross. It is through this ineffable mystery, made up of so much love, that we "will see" forever the glorified body of Christ and his eternal wounds.

So this is the true Lamb of God: he was so on earth and he will continue to be so in the Kingdom of his Father. The eternal wounds of the crucified and resurrected Jesus are the object of our love and adoration, and they will remain so in the Kingdom. They mark the person of Christ forever, and so allow us to recognise him without any risk of mistake when he presents himself to us. They will allow us to love him always with love in adoration in the Kingdom of glory, and this will be our greatest joy, for we will never be separated from this great love: Jesus, Son of God, but son of man. *Who will separate us from the love of Christ?* (Rom 8:35).

Since the wounds of Christ mark his glorified body forever, we can be sure that, in the same way, the sufferings and trials which mark our earthly lives, touching the deepest parts of our beings, will be our most beautiful marks of glory in the Kingdom. If we bear these sufferings, whether bodily or interior sufferings, in union with the Passion of Christ as an offering of himself to his Father, they will shine with glory forever in the Kingdom. In the light of this, we can understand the words of St Paul:

*I consider that the sufferings of this present time
are not worth comparing
with the glory about to be revealed to us.*
(Rom 8:18)

Yes, suffering and difficulties, united to those of Jesus, will mark us with glory forever, just as the body of Christ will bear the marks of his wounds forever.

Love of and adoration for the body and blood of Christ and of his eternal wounds take us always deeper into the mystery of his living person, into the mystery of the love of the Trinity, which is all founded upon love for mankind.

The Immaculate Lamb

For the Jews, the Passover lamb had to be a lamb without blemish: spotless and immaculate. Such a lamb prefigures the Immaculate Lamb, for Christ is the true 'Immaculate' par excellence. The Blessed Virgin Mary rightly bears this title of Immaculate, but owes it to her Son, as she is always to be seen in relation to him. Mary is immaculate because she is the mother of the one who is immaculate.

The one who was to bear the immaculate body of Christ could herself be nothing other than spotless and faultless: immaculate. This similarity between the Son of God and his mother brings us to reflect upon our own future. We carry in us the body and the blood of Christ when we receive him in the Eucharist, but sadly, we do not become immaculate. We are, however, transformed. Our human condition does not allow for a transformation as radical as that of the Blessed Virgin Mary. But Mary is one of us, a human creature. Through a gift from God, through pure grace, she is the 'Immaculate Conception', forever immaculate.

To a far lesser extent during our earthly life, and also through pure grace, Jesus transforms us in him when we receive him in the Eucharist. He is not changed by our wretchedness or our sin: it is we who are changed by his force for life and Resurrection, by his perfection and his saving love. It is Jesus who, every time we receive communion, takes us a little more into himself, right up to the day when he finally calls us to him and we undertake that great passage. We will be stained with wretchedness and sin, but he will call us through death to a life without blemish or fault. We will become pure as the driven snow, in the image of him, for he will clothe us himself with our wedding garments.

The wedding garment is like that of a young bride: it is white and immaculate. It is beautiful and resplendent, not through any virtue of its own but because it has been washed in the blood of the Lamb:

> *Though your sins are like scarlet,*
> *they shall be like snow;*
> *though they are red like crimson,*
> *they shall become like wool.*
> (Isa 1:18)

> *These are they who have come out of the great ordeal;*
> *they have washed their robes*
> *and made them white in the blood of the Lamb.*
> (Rev 7:14)

The Immaculate One will thus make us immaculate so that we may participate in the wedding feast, in the joy of the wedding, or in other words, in the incomparable joy of perfect union.

This is God's wish for each of us once we have been made perfect: the final outcome. This is what we are longing for endlessly in our earthly lives: our own perfect union with the person of Christ.

When we put on the white robe of baptism, or the white robe of Eucharistic communion, we clothe ourselves in Christ. We clothe ourselves in the perfect joy of loving union with Christ. This joy is so immense and so radiant that it is a nuptial joy: *the joy of the wedding of the Lamb.*

Within love in adoration of Jesus Immaculate in the Eucharist there is a nuptial love, or a loving union, which is so strong and so powerful that it will be capable of taking us from this world to the other: from this world to our Father, after having made us whiter than snow.

The white robe is the wedding robe Jesus speaks of in the parable of the Kingdom. No one can enter into the room of the wedding banquet, let alone remain there, if they are not wearing the white robe. This immaculate white robe is the sign of union with God, and is the entry requirement for his Kingdom, where no one can live except in union with God. But anyone who is in union with God is like him:

> *We will be like him,*
> *for we will see him as he IS.*
> (1 Jn 3:2)

In the Kingdom, we will see Jesus in glory clothed in his immaculate robe, for he is both immaculate and resplendent with glory. Everyone who is united with him will be in glory, clothed in white robes. And there will be only one way to get a white robe: we will have to wash it in the blood of the Lamb before it will become spotless and flawless, immaculate.

We will need to have implored God for his pardon as part of our journey of repentance and penitence, carried out with a genuine desire for our hearts to be converted. For those of us who are baptised, this journey is undertaken through the intermediary of the sacraments, especially and most usually through the sacrament of reconciliation. This is why this sacrament is so important.

It is also possible, for certain people, that the robe will be washed by the blood of martyrdom. This will not be their own blood but the blood of the Lamb, for when a Christian gives up his life in the name of Christ, the blood which flows is not only his own but that of Christ, since we are members of his body.

In the same way, all the sufferings of our present life when united with those of Christ, are redemptive, especially if they are invisible to the eyes of the world and even if they do not involve physical injury and the flowing of blood. As part of an ever-deepening progression in penitence and conversion, they unite us to Christ and help to wash our robe in the very suffering of Christ, in the blood of the Lamb. They win for us the wedding robe which marks us as belonging to Christ.

The immaculate wedding robe can only be won for us by the blood of the Lamb. We also need to understand that all eternity will not seem too long a time for us to adore and serve, along with all the angels and elders, the one who will be forever before us as the Immaculate Lamb. For it is as the Lamb of God that he saves us, and in our unceasing adoration we will know and always remember that he is the one who saves, the only one to whom we owe our salvation.

All eternity will not be too long in which to tell him of our love and our gratitude, serving him in adoration. This is the highest form of service, inasmuch as it is the purest and the most heartfelt way in which we can convey to him our love and gratitude.

> *Worthy is the Lamb that was slaughtered*
> *to receive power and wealth and wisdom and might*
> *and honour and glory and blessing!*
> (Rev 5:12)

The wedding joy, a state of overwhelming happiness

The life of adoration leads us little by little, as our life progresses, and as the history of humanity progresses, to the greatest joy or the greatest happiness imaginable. We will know this bliss in the Kingdom: it is the wedding joy, a pure and immaculate joy radiating the splendour of glory.

> *Blessed are those who are invited*
> *to the marriage supper of the Lamb.*
> (Rev 19:9)

Words to this effect are spoken by each priest at each Eucharistic celebration. We can see straightaway the bond between the Eucharist and beatitude: not just one of the many beatitudes, but beatitude or bliss itself, which is none other than the wedding joy. In other words, love and adoration of the Eucharist leads us to this wedding joy which is overwhelming happiness, total bliss.

At several points during the Gospel Jesus compares the Kingdom with a room prepared for a banquet. The most splendid banquet we know is a wedding banquet. Jesus adopts the role of the host: it is his home. His home is a kingdom over which he is the sovereign ruler, and since he is the host, he is the one who issues the invitations.

In order to gain entry into the banqueting room, we have to be invited personally. We must also reply to the invitation, saying we would like to come.

If we accept the invitation we should immediately start to prepare ourselves correctly. Such preparation indicates the bond of friendship and trust, and the joyful gratitude which we would like to demonstrate to the master of the house in going there, and in entering his home. No one can expect to enter into this beautiful home, decked out in preparation for the most fabulous banquet, if they don't feel an inner desire for the company of the inviting host, and an affinity for him, and for all the guests who are so happy to be around him.

If we don't like the host or have been indifferent to him all our lives, we cannot enter into his home: we would be making fun of him and insulting him. In spite of all the joy in his heart and all his great kindness, he could not welcome those who gatecrash, or are tactless, or who come harbouring ill feeling towards him. So he will show this undesirable person the door, for in the wedding room or in the Kingdom, there is nothing but the greatest joy possible. The King has made all the preparations, so that all will be utterly blissful. He cannot allow it to become tainted. In the banqueting room, all the guests will be wearing white robes, the sign of union with Christ: baptismal robe or wedding robe, it all comes to the same thing. The Groom is the one who invites his guests into his home, and there is a personal bond of such intimacy between him and each of his guests that it amounts to a nuptial bond. It is the strongest kind of alliance, and also the deepest and the most tender: an alliance of love.

So, to show us the kind of love he has for each of us, Jesus compares himself with the Groom who invites each child of God into his home, so that each can live there in the most intimate possible union with him. This is perfect joy: this is total bliss.

This bliss we are speaking of is the only true state of blessedness. It is the ultimate happiness, the kind we are and always will be yearning for until we find it in its absolute form in the life of glory. The term 'happiness' would seem more appropriate than that of 'beatitude' or 'blessedness', which carry connotations of inaccessibility and therefore seem to be out of our reach. Furthermore, the idea of remaining in a beatific state does not attract us particularly, suggesting something static. This is why some people are afraid that they will be bored in the endless life awaiting them in heaven. What a terrible shame it is to see things this way, when in fact the love of the Trinity involves intense activity! We will take part in this ever-changing activity, going from one discovery to the next. We will be finding out new things about love, and this is why Jesus promises happiness to those who will inherit the Kingdom, or to those who will see God: this is one and the same thing.

Blessed...,
for theirs is the kingdom of heaven.
(Mt 5:3)

Blessed...,
for they will see God.
(Mt 5:8)

This blessedness, or happiness, revealed and promised to us by Jesus is something so desirable that we should be longing for it. But this happiness does not lie in being poor, or pure, in itself, but rather in the reason for which the poverty or purity is lived. We might say that everything is brought together and contained in this happiness which is greater than any other kind, and which is the happiness of those who are called to the wedding banquet of the Lamb. For the guests at the wedding banquet of the Lamb are taken into the Kingdom: they see God.

This happiness of the wedding guests of the Lamb is offered to us at each Eucharistic celebration. It is renewed for us in the Eucharistic mystery, making us guests at the Lord's Supper here and now. This is a Eucharistic happiness, the joy of communion in the body and blood of Christ. It is the joy of our unceasing adoration of Jesus who saves us. This promise of happiness has already been fulfilled for us, but it exists still in a veiled form. The wedding joy which Jesus speaks of, presenting himself as the Groom who opens the door of the banquet room and invites us in, is a Eucharistic joy. The Eucharist allows us to experience the most intimate union possible with the person of Christ, but we won't experience absolute union until we reach the Kingdom.

This is the life to which we are called, and it is a good thing for us to be more fully aware of the fact. What we call eternal life is nothing other than the experience of love, in adoration, that is in a state of overwhelming joy and gratitude, giving wholehearted thanks of unparalleled beauty. This thanksgiving, this wedding joy, is an intense and total Eucharistic love for the very person of Christ, who will take us deeper and deeper into the mystery of the love of the Trinity, until we reach the heart of our heavenly Father.

The Father is present, too, at the wedding banquet. He is the one who has provided the banqueting room and given his Son the authority to let us in and welcome us there. Through his Son, he has put his Kingdom at our disposition.

Like an attentive father feeling great tenderness in the midst of his family, the Father heads the table at this wedding, delighting in the joy which he has wished for all. He sees the happiness of his Son, his Lamb, a gift of happiness conveyed to all of us, his other children.[2]

All the glory of the Father is here in this accomplished mission of his Son, blossoming in a splendour of glory which is not reserved for God alone, but given to the immense family of the children of God, the "great multitude that no one could count". It is the glory of the Father which reunites this vast family in the banqueting room. The banquet is a Eucharistic feast. Each Eucharistic celebration we participate in is an aspect of this feast in real time for us, but the joy of this wedding banquet is also extended each time we let our gaze rest on Jesus-Eucharist in adoration. What is more, this wedding joy proclaimed in the words of Revelation: *Blessed are those who are invited to the marriage supper of the Lamb* (Rev 19:9) is an anticipation of the Kingdom. The joy is the announcement, and reveals to us the Kingdom.

It is interesting also to note that these words taken from Revelation, the meaning of which is not yet fully clear to us, are repeated in each Eucharistic liturgy. Is this not proof that the glory of Christ lies in having become the Lamb for us, and that his return in glory is linked to the Eucharist? The glory of the Father will burst open, and all his children will be *eucharised*[3] in his Son. This is how love and adoration of the Lamb of God, the Son of the Father, bring us into the heart of the Trinity's love, revealing to us the infinite tenderness of the Father's heart. Love in adoration is love of the Father, the Son and the Holy Spirit.

Lord, show us the Father, and we will be satisfied...
Whoever has seen me has seen the Father.
(Jn 14:8-9)

If only we could see the living Jesus with our own eyes, present in the Eucharist!

If only we knew how to look at him!

May his real presence be offered to us, for our gaze to rest upon!

Through him, we will find the Father: he will show us the Father...

The Holy Spirit, which is the spirit of adoration, will unite in us this love of the Father, through the Son, this love which is one single love:

The love of the living God,
Father, Son and Holy Spirit.

NOTES

1. St Irenaeus.
2. Cf. 'Le Père du Ciel et l'Agneau', *le Mystère de l'Amour vivant*, p. 94.
3. Cf. 'Baptisés et Eucharistiés', *Les Maisons d'adoration,* p.121.

5
A love to be lived in our homes

*"If the family... presents itself
as a domestic sanctuary of the Church."*[1]

The importance of the home in the life of Jesus

The home is a very important place in the life of Jesus, both during his hidden life and his public life. Its role clarifies the significance of the Houses of Adoration needed in this dawning third millennium.

To begin with, even before the coming of Jesus, at the moment of the Annunciation Mary, his mother, is at home. She is not in the Temple, or in any religious centre: she is praying in the silence of her home.

Later, Jesus desired to feel the need for a simple house, and without doubt a poor house: the house at Nazareth. It is thanks to this house, poor as it was, that he lived with his family, the Holy Family, and experienced a family life which was richer than any other, and yet hidden from the world in general.

Those thirty years which make up such a major part of Jesus' earthly life should make us reflect upon the role of a house which seems quite ordinary from the outside, and yet harbours in it the Son of God.

There is great significance in this. It is a lesson without words, but it gives us an example of how to live. In this humble life led by Jesus in Nazareth, silence speaks volumes. The lifestyle he chose reveals profoundly important values.

Jesus, the Word, would express himself later, during the three years of his public life.

The Word of God also spoke to us, but in a different way, during the thirty years of his hidden life. He still speaks to us from this silence of Nazareth, straight into our hearts. He makes us understand the holiness of family life, and the good fortune and happiness of having a roof over our heads, the shelter which even the poorest home offers us. The home is linked to the family: it is the place where we reunite, and so live together as a family.

In addition, this house in which Jesus lived was imprinted with the very holiness of his presence! It was from this humble house in Nazareth that salvation came into the world. It is absolutely amazing to realise that God's great plans were prepared, and are still being prepared, in the silence and poverty of a simple little house.

Although Jesus is often outdoors during his public life, teaching the crowds, he often goes into people's homes, and such episodes crop up throughout his mission. It is interesting to note that each time he goes into someone's home, he invites himself in. The initiative of grace is his, and it is he who decides which house to enter. He is the one who comes to meet us. *I must stay at your house today* (Lk 19:5).

We can see God taking this initiative throughout Jesus' life, and also throughout our own lives. Written into our hearts, this initiative allows us to continue in humility, knowing that nothing comes from us: everything comes from God. Everything is God's gift to us. *I must stay at your house today*: these are marvellous words which teach us, day after day, to abandon ourselves into the hands of God.

So Jesus, who may do as he wishes, goes into the

homes of tax collectors and sinners, into the homes of people who are despised, and of the Pharisees who criticize him so much. *This fellow welcomes sinners and eats with them* (Lk 15:2). Jesus isn't worried about such comments, for it is precisely for such people that he has come: *Those who are well have no need of a physician, but those who are sick* (Mt 9:12).

The Pharisees cannot grasp the idea of the immense liberty of love in which Jesus moves, and into which he wants to draw everyone, especially tax collectors and sinners. For the Pharisees are people who think they are full of integrity but who are, in fact, prisoners of themselves and of all the laws and principles which they have minutely concocted, and which have closed their hearts.

So Jesus is doing something completely new, and during the course of his public life he goes into many homes:

- Zacchaeus' house, into which he clearly invites himself;
- the house at Bethany, where he finds rest
- and is able to gather his strength in the company of his closest friends (Lk 10 and Jn 12);
- the house of Jairus (Lk 8);
- the house at Capernaum, where we see Jesus 'at home' (Mk 2:1);
- the house of the wedding at Cana (Jn 2);
- the house at Emmaus (Lk 24);
- the house of Simon the leper (Mt 26:6 and Mk 14:3);
- the house of Simon the Pharisee (Lk 7:36-48).

There are many other houses visited by Jesus which we could mention. In all of them, Jesus is received with joy. He invites himself into those homes where he knows he will be joyfully received, because hearts open up in his presence, even the hearts of sinners. Such people are overjoyed by his presence, all the more so because they do not believe it possible: they see it not as something they have a right to, but as something to be received as a gift. A gift is an honour conferred, a grace, a sign of attentiveness and even of affection freely given and totally unexpected, especially when we know that we are not worthy of it: "Lord, I am not worthy to receive you."

Jesus' visits to people in their homes are tokens of great affection. When he does this, his gaze rests upon the person, his full attention is given and the person concerned is made to feel worthy. This explains the great joy felt by tax collectors and sinners when Jesus comes to see them.

What is even more important, each time that Jesus comes into a house, his very presence sanctifies it, and changes the hearts of those who live there, converting and transforming them. Their whole lives are changed, as happened with Zacchaeus, Matthew and many others. The presence of Jesus is sanctifying: he is the only source of holiness because only he is holy. *You alone are holy.*

The importance of Houses of Adoration in the new evangelisation

It is important to discover the richness of the presence of Jesus in the family home.

When we think of the life of Jesus during his thirty years hidden inside a house, and during the three years of his public life when he went from house to house, we can see that there is an important spiritual lesson for us.

The Church should imitate Jesus as closely as possible, following the pattern of his actions and behaviour during his earthly life. In doing as Jesus did, the Church will feel herself called to introduce innovations while conserving and living to the full the authentic Tradition, for the benefit of future generations.

Within this movement of renewal which appears throughout the history of the Church, there is a flexibility and an unceasing sense of accommodation which is none other than the spirit of love. There are no fixed rules which should keep the Church prisoner, restricting her to certain specified locations. The Church is called in this third millennium to spread out her feelers, throughout the everyday world, and she cannot do so without going into people's homes, as Jesus did. In the same way that Jesus invited himself into people's homes during his earthly life, so he continues today, offering to come as close as he possibly can to God's children. This is very significant, and we must appreciate its importance for family life and for the life of the Church. Even the terms '*house*' and '*church*' need to be carefully considered, and will be examined below.

The house in the Old Testament

In the Old Testament God presents himself as a Father who takes tender care of individuals and families who have been specially chosen. He inspires them and leads them, revealing his loving plan to them little by little. The term *family* is understood in a very wide sense. God establishes covenants with entire families which bear the name of a House, when this term indicates a line of inheritance. This is the case for example with the House of Jacob, and later with the House of David. God has a plan for these Houses, and this is why he chooses them and consecrates them. He blesses them and loves them especially. With their cooperation, he gradually pursues his plan for the salvation of all mankind: the success of his plan relies upon the continued support of these families with whom a covenant has been made. What God asks them to do is to listen and be obedient to his will, even if the latter sometimes seems utterly inscrutable.

The house at the heart of the New Covenant

In the same way, God is now establishing a covenant with the family, but not just with people from a single family line as in the Old Testament. Today, and ever since the New and Eternal Covenant, he wants to establish a covenant in the love of the Eucharist, in adoration of the body and the blood of Christ.[2] The Houses of Adoration, which God looks upon with such tenderness, draw their inspiration from this new and eternal covenant sealed in the blood of Christ. These families, or rather these homes, are today composed of hearts which are living and beating for their God, in true adoration, in the midst of the everyday world. They can consist of all kinds of people, in different walks of life, and are true churches. If the world around us were not peppered with these living Houses there would not be any churches, in the sense of a place where people gather together for worship. But there wouldn't be any particular churches either, understood in their theological sense, as communities of the People of God entrusted into the care of pastors who are successors to the apostles. In other words, there is no Church without domestic churches.

God's alliance with mankind is not accomplished unless it is experienced by '*Eucharised*' families, that is families living in the living presence of Christ. All those families, all those Houses which feel called to do so should be able to live an intensely Eucharistic life. This is not possible unless they have actual access to the Eucharist, in accordance with conditions clearly defined by the Church. The salvation of both the family and the Church depends upon such an opening up, such an increased self-awareness on the part of the Church.

In favouring the Houses and desiring a New Covenant with them, God in his Son, Jesus-Eucharist, wants to reveal an aspect of his loving plan to us, and his plan of salvation for mankind.

Houses of Adoration, needed so much today

Jesus sanctified the house at Nazareth with his presence, making it holy. Because of him, the family living in this house became the Holy Family.

He sanctified all the houses he visited during his public life, and ensured that his newly-issued call to holiness was heard in each one. How can we hope for the sanctification of families today, except through the same presence of Jesus?

The Magisterium of the Church, particularly the Second Vatican Council, has spoken of domestic churches in the context of the family, which is the living reality making up the foundations of society and of the Church.

Houses of Adoration represent an application of this idea, and are called to achieve its fulfilment by becoming true "domestic sanctuaries of the Church"[3].

In doing this, Houses of Adoration are meeting the real needs of today:

- families are being exposed to negative forces pushing them towards breakdown. Their only strength and support is the living Jesus. The unifying and harmonising presence of Jesus-Eucharist means that they can be houses built upon the rock, which neither wind nor storm will be able to destroy.
- families are overburdened and society hardly helps: current lifestyles impose severe limitations. Mothers with young babies, mothers who have brought life into the world, cannot go even to a nearby parish church to pray to the Lord and adore his special presence in the Blessed Sacrament. They cannot, and should not, leave their children alone at home. On the other hand, they can pray to the Lord and adore him at home. This movement allows them to teach even their very young children about prayer, giving them an example which will help them throughout their lives. This is only one instance, out of many, which shows that when a family prays at home, their home is a church. There are all sorts of families, but the same thing can be said of all of them: wherever there is a soul at prayer, that soul is a church-soul. When will we re-examine our ideas of houses and churches, and see them for what they really are?

Whilst it was the Lord himself who brought about the Houses of Adoration, they are at the same time a response to current lifestyles: they meet the needs of the times and are perfectly adapted to family life.

Being little churches, they allow the Church to spread herself out on the one hand, and to adapt herself to the realities of daily life on the other. Even if they made superhuman efforts, families could not possibly accommodate parish programmes, timetables and set hours which pay no heed to them.

But, by really paying attention to these genuine churches, these Houses, and taking them into account, the Church could accommodate herself to the realities of their daily lives and modes of existence.

People talk a lot about inculturation today. Perhaps it could start with this.

Domestic churches, extensions of the Church into the world around us

Our idea of 'church' needs to be expanded so that the Church may grow.

We tend to think too much of the church as a building made of bricks and mortar, a place where we worship and gather together. It is true that the *Ecclesia* is the called assembly of God, and that these places for collective gathering play a pivotal role in the life of the Church. There is still much to do before they will truly develop into centres of life and vitality, but the domestic churches can help in this by bringing a new missionary impulse to parishes and to the local churches.

From now on, it will be helpful to remember that an assembly is made up of people and families. These people do not live in the presbytery of their parish, but in their homes. There would be no *Ecclesia* without the people who make it up, nor without all the *ecclesiola*: the little churches.

The homes of all those people who disappear after each Mass are places full of life and love, and are in themselves the Church. They are genuine churches, places of shelter for the children of God.

Houses of Adoration, a Eucharistic vocation in the everyday world

The full blossoming of a House of Adoration's vocation as a domestic church is brought about by the person of Christ in his Eucharist. For the Church is founded on the body of Christ.

In every House of Adoration, life revolves entirely around love of the body and blood of Christ: life is Eucharistic. But there is no Eucharist without a priest. A House of Adoration, living in the love of the Eucharist, is by definition bound up with the vocation of priesthood. This does not mean however that the priest should live in the house: he cannot, and neither should he. The priest lives in the presbytery. But he knows his parishioners: a good shepherd knows all of his children. He can vouch for an individual or a family, recognise a genuine vocation for a House of Adoration, and help those concerned to live the Eucharistic spirituality involved. The priest can help in many ways:

- through his own example of life centred around the love of the Eucharist, and shared with his parishioners;

- by helping those who are entrusted to him to develop, and arrive at a deeper understanding of, the sacramental life and the interior life;
- by developing the life of adoration.

The new approach would involve making Jesus-Eucharist really accessible, little by little, to those families called to live this life of adoration:

- by allowing Jesus-Eucharist to be really close to them;
- by entrusting Jesus-Eucharist to them, in their homes, as Jesus was entrusted to Mary and Joseph in their home.

This cannot be done unless every confidence is placed in these families as being true domestic churches.

The presence of Jesus within a home develops the faith, hope and love of each family member. It allows each person to live as in the times of Christ's earthly life, and to repeat these beautiful words of St John:

What we have heard,
what we have seen with our eyes,
what we have looked at...
concerning the word of life...
we declare to you.
(1 Jn 1:1-3)

How can we burn with love for Jesus without his presence, without him being close to us?

It seems to me that the family is dying because people cannot really come close to Jesus. In his great loving tenderness, he has provided us with the solution by setting up a new kind of relationship with his people.

He is the one who is proposing to come into our homes. He is inviting himself.

How can we ignore this burning desire of Christ?

It is the same desire as he had during his earthly life: he wants to be close to mankind. The only thing that has changed is the nature of his presence: now it is Eucharistic.

The Eucharist is entrusted into the care of priests. During the feeding of the five thousand, Jesus said the following surprising words to his disciples:

They need not go away;
you give them something to eat.
(Mt 14:16)

The disciples were ready to send the crowds away, so that they could find their own food.

Send the crowds away
so that they may go into the villages
and buy food for themselves.
(Mt 14:15)

Jesus didn't want this. He wanted the Bread of Life to be entrusted to priests so that, far from locking it up, they would distribute it: *You give them something to eat.*

The equivalent meaning of this today is: Give them the Bread of Life which they are hungering after. Family access to the Eucharist is a vitally important issue for the life of the Church, and must be discussed.

All the necessary safeguards and precautions will be truly present in the form of links with the parish, and therefore supervision by the priest and by the bishop. Houses of Adoration can thus be an integral part of the Church, as domestic churches and true sanctuaries of the Church within the home.

The life of adoration as suggested in this book cannot be fully lived unless Jesus is close to those who belong to him.

We could each adore the Blessed Sacrament in the home no matter what the time, and especially late into the evening or during the night.

Many souls, many families are calling for this presence of Jesus and are waiting for it, full of hope.

The Church is like a mother stretching out her two long arms to guard and protect, and gather to herself, the little churches of our homes. These two long arms are like two solid flying buttresses, giving the Universal Church stability and strength. The Church cannot remain upright if there is a gap between her and the buttresses supporting her sides.

Our living reality is made up of constant communication and interchange, and our Houses of Adoration, or little churches, exist only through the maternal protection of the Church. They are born of her. There is a vital and complementary relationship between the two, for both belong to the same whole: the same body which the Holy Spirit is acting on, so that it may breathe with both lungs.

On a practical level, Houses of Adoration are clearly homes within a parish, within a given diocese: they are integrated into the Church, and part of her. They are little churches, true extensions of the Church within the world of everyday life, and are part and parcel of the Church, attached not through obligation but through true love of the Church of Christ. We can see that the Lord himself is now silently and patiently opening our hearts to the idea of this new pathway.

Houses of Adoration, forerunners of the Holy City

It would seem that we are witnessing a time of preparation for the Holy City, for the transfigured Church will be the Holy City described in the Book of Revelation. But there will be no temple in the Holy City:

> *I saw no temple in the city...*
> (Rev 21:22)

This means that the presence of God is not restricted to a particular location. The Lord in his glory is offering to be with us, to come to us himself.

To prepare us for this time to come, the Lord wants to come and live with us in our homes. He is as yet still hiding his glory, within the Eucharist, until the day comes when he will show it to us.

The Holy City is under construction at this very moment, being made up of a multitude of homes. A city does not consist of just one building: it is the whole which is the sum of all the homes which are its constituent parts. A city is also, at the same time, made up of a multitude of people of all kinds and from all walks of life:

> *After this I looked,*
> *and there was a great multitude*
> *that no one could count...*
> (Rev 7:9)

This is so reassuring for us, so full of hope and joy!

So let us prepare our homes, let us create holy homes which are truly little churches, until the whole earth is filled with the one and only Church of Christ.

NOTES

1. Vatican II, *Apostolicam Actuositatem*, no. 11 (on the Apostolate of Lay People).
2. Cf. *le Mystère de l'Amour vivant,* p. 326.
3. Cf. Vatican II, *Apostolicam Actuositatem*, no. 11.